The 13 Critical Tasks

An Inside-Out Approach to Solving More Gun Crime

by

Pete Gagliardi

ISBN: 978-0-615-39145-8

Forensic Technology WAI Inc.
5757 Cavendish Boulevard, Suite 200
Cote St. Luc, Quebec, Canada H4W 2W8
Telephone: +1 514-489-4247 Canada/USA Toll free +1-888-984-4247
Fax: +1 514-485-9336
E-mail: info@contactft.com
Web site: www.forensictechnology.com

This book is dedicated to all victims of firearm violence and their families, all men and women of law enforcement, the forensic scientists, prosecutors, and court and corrections personnel who are at the front lines, dealing with armed criminals and the aftermath of their violent acts; to all public administrators, policy makers, and private sector businesses that support those on the front lines by providing the guidance, resources, and tools needed to address violent crime; and last, but not least, to every one of us who is seeking a more peaceful and just way of life.

Contents

Contents

Contents

Contents

Contents

Acknowledgments

Thank you to the many law enforcement and forensic agencies and practitioners who lead the way in designing and implementing the best practices described in this book. Thank you to the researchers whose work is highlighted herein. Thank you to the men and women at Forensic Technology whose dedication to innovation has led to the introduction of new and groundbreaking tools for law enforcement.

Thanks to the Core 13 Critical Tasks Development Working Group: Dr. Anthony Braga, Harvard University; Cresha Cason, Patty Xenos, Mike McLean, Forensic Technology; Catherine Doherty, Boston Police Department; Michelle Kuehner, Allegheny County Coroner's Office; John O'Neil, the men and women at Forensic Technology; and Dr. Glenn Pierce, Northeastern University.

Forensic Technology would also like to acknowledge the contributions made by the U.S. Department of Justice, the Bureau of Alcohol, Tobacco, Firearms and Explosives, the Boston Police Department, the New York Police Department, the Los Angeles Police Department, the SKL - Kriminaltekniska of Sweden, the Kriminalpolitisentralen of Norway, the Rigspolitichefen of Denmark, the South African Police Service, the New South Wales Police Force, and the many others who have enlightened us along the way.

A special thanks to Dale Armstrong, Bill Casey, Laurie Van Deusen, Wayne Hoffman, Ed Jachimowicz, Pat Maney, the NIBIN Team, Virginia O'Brien, Nannette Rudolf, Alex D'Atri, Chris Sadowski, Jim Stephenson, Neil Van Niekerk, and John Ward for the discussions and actions in support of the concept of Regional Crime Gun Protocols.

This book never would have been possible without the support and assistance of Patrick Doyon, Andre Demers, Marlene Reed, and Anthony Gagliardi.

Finally, thank you to Robert Walsh and René Bélanger of Forensic Technology whose generosity has allowed us to print and distribute this publication at no charge.

What People Are Saying About
The 13 Critical Tasks

"If you care anything at all about guns and crime, you have to read Pete Gagliardi's new book. Don't just put it on the shelf. Read it. Read it again and again until you need a new one. Gagliardi writes in an engaging style and clearly lays out everything you need to know about the mechanics and solutions to investigating gun crimes. Although he eschews mucking about in the social issues of crime and gun control—with good reason—this must be read by those who do. So many people who do care about that side and who fancy themselves as "experts" actually know virtually nothing about the down and dirty details of gun crimes and how real detectives solve them. If five stars is tops, I give this book a ten!"—Tom Diaz, Writer

"This book demonstrates the extraordinary crime solving potential of ballistics technology. A firearm in the hands of a criminal is a powerful destructive force yet that the same firearm can also be the Achilles heel that exposes the criminal to detection, arrest and conviction. The full utilization of the tools and best practices identified in this book should become the staples of professional policing that make our communities safer by targeting armed criminals."—Bradley Buckles, former Director–Bureau of Alcohol, Tobacco, Firearms and Explosives (ATF)

"Thousands are killed by gunfire each year and hundreds of thousands more are threatened or injured in robberies and assaults. In *The 13 Critical Tasks*, Pete Gagliardi lays out a practical set of ideas, supported by real-world examples, which can help cities address their gun crime problems now. He clearly shows that the harm done by armed criminals can be mitigated through the comprehensive collection and analysis of crime gun information and by achieving balance in the people, processes, and technologies mobilized to apprehend repeat gun offenders. This book is a must-have for law enforcement executives everywhere."—Dr. Anthony A. Braga, Harvard University

What People Are Saying About
The 13 Critical Tasks

About This Book

This book is about reducing gun related violence.

It is about targeting the **armed criminal** who fired his gun yesterday, shot it again today, and most probably will shoot it again tomorrow.

It is about developing better ways to identify armed criminals who misuse guns and do harm to others, so they can be brought to justice and removed from the communities upon which they prey.

This is not a book about the social or economic drivers of violent crime. Recognizing that society must work on addressing the underlying social causes of violent crime, it must in the meantime relentlessly pursue every armed criminal who has engaged in a violent act.

The intent of this book is to share the author's some 40 years of experience and expertise in the firearm investigation and ballistics technology arenas.

It is the sincere hope of the author and Forensic Technology, the self-publisher, that others who are interested in improving the way in which firearm crimes are investigated may benefit from the information in this book and from the time saved by not having to retrace the author's steps.

This book advocates the presumptive approach to the investigation of crimes involving the misuse of firearms and makes a call to action.

The information in this book is based on a combination of personal lessons learned and the best practices developed by others. The book's value stems from the unique opportunity that the author and the self-publisher have had to collect information from their almost daily interaction with the foremost law enforcement and forensic experts from around the world.

This book focuses on taking the "presumptive approach" to the investigation of crimes involving the misuse of firearms. This approach presumes that every gun generates information which, when well managed, can be of significant value in helping to solve gun crimes. The book tackles this complex issue by dividing it into a series of logically-arranged tasks involving people, processes, and technology. Each task is explained in terms of why it is important, what it entails, and how it is being implemented most efficiently and effectively by others.

While it takes an understanding of all of the tasks to fully implement an integrated and sustainable firearm crime reduction program, this book has been designed to be a flexible and ready reference for those readers interested in just a particular task or group of tasks. Since this book may not necessarily be read in sequence—as one reads chapter after chapter in a novel—some information has been repeated in various chapters for clearer understanding.

Prologue

The young ATF[1] agent had been on the job for roughly four years when he learned a lesson that would forever change the way he saw crime. This change altered the way in which he approached his life's work and, more importantly, would later help shape the way in which gun crime is investigated around the world. The paradigm he helped shift is still used today—30 years later.

It wasn't so much an epiphany, but more a series of escalating lessons learned during the course of a not so ordinary murder investigation conducted in New Haven, Connecticut, in 1980.

The shooting took place one Friday night, about two weeks before Christmas. The victim, Perry Farnham, was a man who had been cooperating with police. In Hamden, a city contiguous to New Haven, police were investigating the theft of over a half-million dollars worth of home heating oil. Farnham ran an environmental cleanup business located along side the Ferry Street Bridge. An employee returning late from an oil spill cleanup found him dead on the concrete floor of the garage bay—his body lying next to one of the parked tanker trucks.

Nobody saw the shooters, but there was plenty of physical evidence: fired bullets and cartridge cases. A series of bullets was recovered from one of the garage bay walls and more were later removed from Farnham's body during the autopsy. Expended cartridge cases littered the garage bay floor and were also collected. None of this was particularly unusual, given the circumstances.

The evidence, including the brass on the floor, was sent to Ballistics for examination. There, experts would examine the unique markings left on the recovered fired ammunition components. When ammunition is discharged, the components—bullets and cartridge cases—come into forced contact with some of the gun's internal surfaces. The nature of the contact is such that the marks left on certain parts inside the gun during the manufacturing process become imprinted into surfaces of the fired bullets and cartridge cases.

---

[1] Bureau of Alcohol, Tobacco, Firearms and Explosives, U.S.A.

By the next morning, an enormous amount of information began to pour out of the Ballistics Unit. Forming opinions exclusively from the examinations of the fired bullets and cartridge cases, the firearm examiners were able to tell detectives that the murder weapon was most probably an RPB Industries, model SM-10, .45 Auto/ACP pistol—the semiautomatic cousin to the MAC 10 fully automatic submachine gun. The RPB pistol could be readily converted to a machine gun and lots of people knew how to do it; with simple hand tools, and a few modifications, the gun could sustain full automatic fire with a single pull of the trigger. This fact, coupled with a crime scene photo depicting the telltale staccato pattern of the bullet holes in the garage bay wall, piqued the interest of the young ATF agent.

ATF firearm experts in Washington, D.C., would add an interesting piece to the puzzle: from the rifling pattern on the bullets, they would conclude that the murder weapon was one of about three thousand that had been made since RPB Industries began using a newly designed barrel configuration only three months prior to the shooting. This actionable information was the driver of the investigative strategy to try and identify all of the RPB, model SM-10, .45 Auto/ACP pistols with the new barrel design that entered the state of Connecticut. After all, the odds were not that bad; 3,000 guns were made and with 50 states, just how many could have possibly been sold at retail in a little state like Connecticut? If necessary, the next strategic step would be to expand the search outward from Connecticut to other states.

That step was never taken.

The good thing about a federal agency like ATF is that it has offices strategically located across the United States and in other countries as well. The best thing about ATF is that it has some outstanding investigators working in those offices.

ATF and the New Haven PD detectives launched a "collateral investigation request" for a records inspection to be conducted at the premises of the primary distributor for RPB Industries, located in Georgia. The request for assistance went to the ATF Atlanta office, not far from where the principal distributor was located. In a matter of days, detectives had an answer to their question "how many guns of the type used in the New Haven murder could have been shipped to Connecticut?" The answer was three—and all to the same gun dealer.

The young ATF agent and a New Haven PD detective visited the gun dealer and were able to identify the three purchasers of the guns in question by relying on the information contained on the outside of the guns: make, model, and serial number.

At one point during the investigation, one co-conspirator tried to reassure the other that they could not get caught. As he tried to make the point that the police had nothing to go on, he said during a conversation which was electronically monitored and recorded: **"they got nothing—all they got is some brass on the floor"**. That may have been the attitude of some criminals toward the forensic science capabilities of the police back in 1980—but even back then it would prove to be a huge miscalculation.

The lesson learned here was to approach every crime committed with a gun with the presumption that every crime gun and piece of ballistic evidence can provide actionable crime-solving information of tactical and strategic value.

Some might call this lesson learned some 30 years ago an obvious one. Perhaps, but then why is it that something so obvious still remains undone or disorganized in most places around the world today?

Without a doubt, the police and forensic agencies that take this presumptive approach are among the most successful in dealing with firearm related violent crime.

Prologue

The Presumptive Approach: Every Crime Gun Has a Story to Tell

Why Is the Presumptive Approach Needed?

Firearm related violence is often cyclical and repetitive. Harvard Professor Anthony Braga, who has conducted a great deal of research in this area, said recently: "Street gangs tend to get caught up in cycles of retribution. One shooting or one homicide tends to beget a series of homicides..."[2]

This type of repetitive violence has severe social consequences in terms of human suffering and the fear that it generates among those who live within its reach. It also has drastic economic impact in terms of the cost of crime to society in general and, more specifically, on the socioeconomic structure of the affected neighborhood. The fact is that people avoid doing business and socializing in areas where firearm violence is reported to be prevalent.

The reports from around the world are all very similar as to the belief that crime involving the misuse of firearms is on the rise, particularly involving young people who feel that they are disrespected "on the street" and criminal gangs who operate across both regional and national boundaries.

What Is the Forecast?

A balance of diverse solutions ranging from addressing the underlying social and economic causes to improving the criminal justice system and law enforcement must be implemented. The purpose of this book is to delineate two points that are integral to these solutions:

---

[2] Interviewed by Molly Lanzarotta on March 21, 2006.

- Valuable information for law enforcement use can be extracted from crime guns and related evidence.

- People, processes, and technology solutions are available to help sustain the production of actionable information from this data which can help police solve and prevent gun related crimes.

The 13 Critical Tasks

Definition: The presumptive approach to the investigation of crimes involving firearms presumes that there is an abundance of data both inside (which is transferred to fired bullets and cartridge cases) and outside every crime gun. When fully exploited, this data can be used to generate actionable information of tactical and strategic crime solving value.

Valuable crime solving technology exists today. For example, automated ballistic identification systems, like **IBIS®**[3], can help police process a firearm that has been seized for cause during a routine car stop to a series of prior murders. Fired bullets and cartridge cases collected at one crime scene can be linked to a series of previous crimes. The police can then combine and leverage the bits of information known about each crime. With more "pieces of the puzzle" in hand, police can see a clearer picture of what transpired, helping them find a suspect more quickly. Automated ballistic identification systems have been carefully studied and have proven to provide a valuable service in helping to solve gun related crimes, particularly crimes lacking suspects or leads. When networked, these systems enable the quick searching of multiple ballistic databases across local, regional, and international jurisdictions, helping to produce leads that would have otherwise remained undetected.

Another example is firearm information management systems that are used to track the life cycle of a firearm. These systems allow police to trace the history of a crime gun. Commonly referred to as "crime gun

---

[3] Integrated Ballistics Identification System, created by Forensic Technology.

tracing", this tracing process can provide leads to investigators which help identify armed criminals and firearm traffickers. It also helps police and policy makers accurately identify patterns and trends in illegal gun markets in order to design new enforcement strategies and tactics.

From practical experience, one thing is clear, unless we are able to collect and analyze accurate information about the criminal misuse of firearms across a city, state, province, or country, we cannot begin to apply effective law enforcement tactics and design new strategies to address the problem. Without this critical information gathered in a timely manner, we are destined to use inefficient work processes resulting in misdirected and wasted resources. Without timely information from which we can generate actionable intelligence, we are left blindfolded, with one hand tied behind our backs.

With witnesses generally reluctant to come forward in shooting cases—especially gang related ones—the most important thing for police is to have actionable information that can be acted upon.

What Information Is Available for Solving Gun Crimes?

Generally, the information falls into two broad categories: crime related and non-crime related.

Crime related information triggers the moment the firearm is unlawfully possessed or used to commit a crime. It includes fired ammunition components—the bullets and cartridge cases discharged during the commission of the crime. Crime related information also includes other forensic data, such as DNA, fingerprints, and hairs and fibers which can help police identify the unlawful gun possessor.

Non-crime related information is collected according to the law during the course of regulated commerce associated with the manufacture, distribution, sale, and transfer of firearms. Historically, policy makers have viewed regulatory controls as a means of preventing or minimizing the misuse of firearms. The regulatory systems that support these controls collect an enormous amount of information which can also be of significant value to police in developing tactics and strategies to deal with gun related crimes.

It is the capacity of law enforcement to lawfully and efficiently access this non-crime related information which provides the ability to trace the history of legal transactions in what is commonly referred to as a gun trace pursuant to a criminal investigation.

It is the ability of law enforcement to legally and efficiently access this non-crime information which provides the ability to trace the history of legal transactions in what is commonly referred to as a gun trace pursuant to a criminal investigation. However, once the trace has been conducted the trace information then falls into the category of crime related information and must be efficiently and effectively managed in order for it to be of tactical or strategic law enforcement value in gun related investigations.

Some countries are taking steps to capture ballistic data from non-crime related guns as part of the firearm regulatory process. This data becomes an additional identifier to be linked with the other non-crime related information required in the normal course of legal firearm commerce.

Where Is the Information?

The information is found in two places: inside the gun and outside the gun.

From the inside of the gun comes ballistic data in the form of unique markings left on fired ammunition components by the internal working parts of a gun.

From the outside comes identifying data in the form of make, model, and serial number that can be used to track the transactional history of the gun. For example, every gun made in the U.S. since 1968, by law, must bear certain identifying information that is visible on the outside, such as the name and location of the manufacturer and a unique serial number. In addition, gun manufacturers and dealers must keep certain records documenting their firearm acquisition and disposition transactions in the regular course of their business. Performing what is called a crime gun trace, police can trace the history of a recovered crime gun by backtracking along the "paper trail" of firearm transactions from the day the gun was manufactured to its first retail sale.

In addition, other valuable forensic data, such as DNA, fingerprints, and trace evidence, which can help police identify the gun possessor, can be found on the surface bearing areas of the firearm and ammunition components.

How Can the Information Be of Value, Both Tactically and Strategically?

Tactical information is generally viewed for the purposes of this discussion as information that is generated over the short term which has immediate relevance and value to a particular event or series of related events.

Strategic information is generally viewed here as information that is collected over the long term which can be used to identify patterns and trends for quantification and targeting purposes, informed decision making, and resource alignment.

The information from inside and outside a gun can have crime solving tactical value. For example, ballistic data from the inside can link a gang member's gun to a crime or series of crimes.

It can also link crimes in which the same firearm was used so that police can leverage the information known about each crime to generate additional investigative leads.

Crime gun trace data from outside the gun, such as a serial number, can be used tactically to help police identify the first legal purchaser of the firearm, which in turn can lead them to the person who misused it in a criminal act. It can also be used strategically to identify patterns and trends in crime gun markets. DNA and fingerprint data from outside the gun can help police identify the actual possessor when there is more than one possibility. For example, consider the common police motor vehicle stop in which a crime gun is seized from under the front seat of a car occupied by four people. The question is: who actually possessed the firearm—one, two, or all four? Obviously, this information is important in sustaining a conviction when the possession of the firearm is unlawful. However, if the ballistic data was to tie the gun to a previous murder, the answer to the question of possession rises to an even higher level of importance.

This issue of tactical and strategic information of value gathered when employing the presumptive approach will be discussed further in upcoming chapters.

Key Considerations

- Ensure that there is a firearm regulatory structure in place at any government level whereby information about the legal commerce in firearms is recorded and accessible to law enforcement for crime gun tracing.

- Consider whether the law enforcement and forensic capacity exist to collect and process all of the available crime related and non-crime related information from inside and outside the gun, such as ballistics, ballistic networks, DNA, fingerprints, hair, fibers, trace evidence, and firearm transaction records.

- Determine whether there are efficient and effective protocols and processes in place to collect, manage, and share the input and output information in a sustainable and legally appropriate way.

- Consider whether the processes that are in place are institutionalized up, down, and across affected organizations.

- Consider to what degree the presumptive approach has been used. At a minimum, electronic crime gun tracing and automated ballistic testing should be done.

- Determine whether the information generated through the presumptive approach is being used for both tactical and strategic purposes.

Summary

The Most Important Thing: Using the presumptive approach to the investigation of crimes involving firearms. It presumes that there is an abundance of data inside and outside every crime gun. When fully exploited, this data can be used to generate actionable information of tactical and strategic crime solving value.

<u>The Next Step:</u> The next chapter discusses the important role that technology can play in helping to sustain the presumptive approach and generate substantial crime solving and prevention benefits.

2
Chapter

Technology Helps Sustain Processes

Why Adopt and Adapt?

Stakeholders must adopt and adapt to provide people with the tools needed to help increase efficiency and effectiveness as well as sustain processes.

People will always be the principal driver in any crime reduction solution. However, people can become more efficient and effective through the use of good processes supported by technology.

Consider the science of firearm examination or, as some call it, forensic ballistics. One of the key processes in the presumptive approach to firearm crime investigation is forensic firearm examination in order to exploit the ballistic data that is generated from inside the gun.

For the past 80 years, police have relied upon forensic ballistics to link fired bullets and cartridge cases to each other and to crime guns that were in police custody. The court-tested theory has remained unchanged for nearly 80 years: every gun leaves unique microscopic markings on the surface areas of fired bullets and cartridge cases. Experts use comparison microscopes to compare these markings in an effort to identify similarities that positively link them together, subsequently concluding that the ammunition components were fired from the same gun.

However, up until about 15 years ago, the process of examining ballistic evidence was a very labor intensive and time consuming task.

Only firearm examiners could perform analyses and the work was often reactive in nature. It typically involved a situation in which police had a gunshot victim, a suspect, and a smoking gun. The firearm examiner's job was to validate if the bullet taken from the victim was fired from the smoking gun found in the hand of the suspect and to be prepared to testify to that fact in court.

The proactive nature of the forensic ballistics discipline was somewhat limited by the nature of the work, which involves infinite combinations of microscopic markings pitted against the human capacity for memory. It would happen, from time-to-time, that a firearm examiner would remember a particular mark or series of marks that stood apart from the others for some reason, but this was more of an exception than the rule. Most often, the proactive use of the discipline involved hunches. For example, a detective who had just recovered a gun from a suspect had a hunch that it may have been used in a particular murder. The detective would ask the firearm examiner to test fire the gun and compare the test fired samples to the fired bullet and cartridge case evidence on file that was collected from the murder scene.

For many years this was the way in which things were done. It was an impossible and improbable task for a ballistics lab with large firearm evidence caseloads to be able to sustain the comparison of every piece of ballistic evidence coming into the lab against every other piece in the entire inventory. It was impossible because of resource and time constraints and it was improbable that the resources would have been devoted to a manual process without the aid of technology.

The preceding chapter concluded that the ability to sustain the types of processes required in taking the presumptive approach when investigating gun crime is the key to crime solving success. Technology can help people sustain these processes.

How Can We Adopt and Adapt?

Through technology advancements in automated ballistic identification systems, ballistic information sharing networks, firearm tracing systems, automated fingerprint identification systems and other areas as well.

Automated Ballistic Identification Systems

In the early 1990s, the manual processes of forensic ballistics analysis received a boost of speed and sustainability with the introduction of automated ballistic identification technology with systems like IBIS and Drugfire[4].

Leveraging the power of computers, ballistic imaging technology like IBIS captures the digital images of the unique markings that are left on fired bullets and cartridge cases by the internal working parts of a gun and then stores this information in a database. With lightning speed, the technology is able to search a particular image of a bullet or cartridge case against the inventory of other images in the database and rank them in order of the highest likelihood of a match for subsequent confirmation by an expert. The latest IBIS technologies like **IBIS®** TRAX-3D™ process information in both two and three dimensions, providing new and more powerful data matching, visualization, and comparison tools.

IBIS technology's crime solving value has been clearly established through rigorous academic and scientific study. IBIS and NIBIN[5] have been ardently endorsed by the International Association of Chiefs of Police (IACP) and by government leaders and policy makers around the world.

The benefits of adopting new technology in support of the presumptive approach far surpass speed alone. Technology can bust barriers—helping law enforcement personnel sweep through backlogs and delays to more quickly identify shooters before they have a chance to shoot and kill again.

Also, because IBIS technology enables technicians to generate crucial lab work that can be used by the expert firearm examiners, there are cost efficiencies to be realized with technicians versus firearm examiners in terms of lower training time and pay requirements. The time needed to train a technician is far less than the time needed to train a firearm examiner. Technicians performing data entry and other tasks help support

---

[4] Drugfire was a technology developed under the FBI. In 1999, ATF and the FBI agreed to select IBIS as the technology standard for the National Integrated Ballistic Information Network (NIBIN) and the Drugfire systems were replaced by IBIS.

[5] NIBIN: The National Integrated Ballistic Information Network. ATF has made NIBIN available to law enforcement agencies in every major metropolitan area in the U.S. The grid that connects nationwide IBIS users is called NIBIN. Currently there are almost 200 NIBIN partners (mostly state, county, and city law enforcement agencies or crime laboratories) in possession of IBIS systems at over 200 locations. ATF administers the high speed network over which the units communicate. [Source: Police Chief Magazine, December, 2009]

the experts and keep them focused on the more productive, higher level outputs. The efficiencies gained by the use of technicians also make it possible for a lab to sustain the comprehensive imaging of more ballistic data and the generation of more proactive investigative leads.

Technology can also help sustain higher levels of efficiency and effectiveness when users are able to adapt to the changes that the new technology requires and adopt new processes that help maximize the technology's benefits, just like the police have done in Los Angeles, New York, Boston, Chicago, Phoenix, West Palm Beach, Orlando, Pittsburgh, and in other countries and continents, such as South Africa, the United Kingdom, Australia, Israel, India, and Europe (INTERPOL: The International Criminal Police Organization).

Doreen Hudson, Assistant Director of the Los Angeles Police Crime Lab, shows us how she adapted to change and adopted new processes in her lab. After adapting to the use of ballistics technology in her lab, she conducted a study to determine if she needed to adopt new work processes centered on the technology. She wanted to determine what factor or factors should drive the ballistic comparison work of the Ballistics Unit. Should the lab continue to depend on the old ways of doing business in which a police officer would request a ballistic comparison based on received information or on a hunch that a gun was used in a particular crime? Or, would it be better to let the technology identify possible ballistic matches and have the firearm examiners focus their time on making those comparisons and confirmations?

When operating on hunches, her study concluded that her firearm examiners were producing positive information for investigators only about 30 percent of the time (information that linked evidence from two different crimes scenes or a piece of ballistic evidence to the gun that fired it). This is not to say that the firearm examiners were not doing good work—they certainly were. The problem, as Ms. Hudson saw it, was that 70 percent of the time when following up on hunches, the firearm examiners were confirming, according to old police jargon, a "negative result". In other words, they were spending their valuable time proving that the gun under examination was <u>not</u> the murder weapon. While this type of information could be useful in eliminating a suspect or a specific gun amongst a group of suspected guns, the reality was that it did little to help detectives advance their investigations of shooting crimes.

With limited resources and evidence from an explosion of violent gang activity pouring into her lab, Ms. Hudson tried to find a better way. She conducted a study whereby the IBIS technology was linked to the NIBIN database in order to drive the lab's casework. The premise was simple, all ballistic evidence from shootings and all test fires from guns seized during police investigations would be imaged into the IBIS systems in her lab and then searched against the NIBIN database for possible matches. If matches were found, her team of firearm examiners would contact the detectives involved and follow-up on the cases, if appropriate. When Ms. Hudson compared the performance measures of this study, she reported that when using technology to guide her processes the firearm examiners were providing positive information to detectives well over 70 percent of the time—a complete 180 degree reversal from what the hunches had produced. Relying on the benefits of technology to drive the LAPD's ballistics work, Ms. Hudson later saw that 70 percent positive result statistic increase to 80 percent.

The data networking capability of IBIS represents an enormous benefit that essentially changes the rules of the game. Many barriers to the presumptive approach can be surmounted through the use of wide area data communication networks.

Consider this all-too-common true life example: Police in New Haven, Connecticut, recover a 9 millimeter pistol from a street-corner dealer during a drug bust. Considering the fact that there have been many drug related shootings in the neighborhood where the pistol was recovered, the police officers would like the firearm checked through NIBIN. Many cities like New Haven rely upon services provided by state or county crime labs which serve a number of police agencies throughout the region. Therefore, police officers must generally perform the following steps in order to have a firearm like the pistol in the example above checked against NIBIN:

- Complete the agency's process for taking property into custody.

- Indicate that the pistol is being sent to the state crime regional lab for examination.

- Prepare the paperwork for transmitting the pistol to the lab and for the request for forensic services.

- Preserve the integrity of possible evidence on or in the pistol and package it for transportation to the lab.

- Drive or ship the package to the lab.

- The lab must then receive the package and verify the inventory of its contents.

- The lab follows its process for opening up a package and taking custody of the pistol.

- The lab assigns a priority to the examination and the pistol sits in the evidence storage area awaiting its turn for examination.

- The time eventually arrives for the examination to take place and the pistol is processed according to the protocol of the lab, not only for the specific check requested by the police officers.

- Most often, firearms are examined in their entirety; this includes a variety of measurements, such as various barrel dimensions, class characteristics, safety mechanisms, and trigger pull requirements.

- Firearms must also be processed for DNA and latent fingerprints.

- Eventually the pistol will be test fired and the test fires will be entered and searched against NIBIN.

- The person to whom the case is assigned will prepare a lab report to document all processing that was conducted on the firearm and will then forward it to an internal review process.

- After the report reviews are completed, the evidence will be released and a report forwarded to the requester.

- The requester will have to make arrangements to collect the evidence and have it transported back to the police department.

- The evidence must be re-entered into the agency property inventory record and storage area.

At best, this process can take weeks; it will most likely take months and maybe even years.

The question that must be asked is: How long do these fifteen steps take to execute in your jurisdiction? Do not believe any answer that is unaccompanied by hard data collected in an independently monitored time trial. If a time trial has not been conducted—then conduct one. Discussions or decisions on current performance outputs, such as time, must be based on fact rather than speculation.

Back to the New Haven example above: consider the consequences if the lab report returned to New Haven indicated negative results—no matches to any evidence in the national database. All that effort was expended just to produce a negative results report. This would only happen a few times before a police officer thinks twice about going through all this trouble again.

Cops take gambles every day out on the street and they quickly become masters at running and playing the odds. They may quickly tire of jumping through somebody else's hoops only to receive reports with negative results. If there's no shortcut, they may simply avoid the situation. Labs look at these issues too and use such feedback when establishing casework priorities. **Guns that are not immediately associated with crimes at the time of recovery are generally given the lowest priority by labs—plain and simple.**

Everyone loses if the police and crime scene technicians cease submitting firearm evidence to the lab. The cops lose the benefit of the useful information to be gained through the presumptive approach, the labs lose their purpose, justice is ill-served, and the public suffers. The only winners are the criminals. This state of affairs is likely more common than many people may think. It is commonly known in the law enforcement community that there are many federal, state, and local law enforcement agencies which do not send all of the guns that they recover to the lab for ballistic testing even when there is a ballistics technology networked database to search against. Why? Most probably because the process required for doing so is bureaucratic, labor intensive, or otherwise unsustainable.

While street cops and agents hate paperwork-laden bureaucratic processes —and this is understandable—they appreciate anything that can really aid them in their crime solving missions.

What if the lab report in the New Haven scenario had indicated a positive result; that the pistol that was submitted for test-firing was actually linked to one or more crimes in the neighborhood? This fact would translate into "points on the board", but only if the turnaround time was such that the information represented a fairly fresh investigative lead for police to follow. The longer the turnaround time, the less potential value of the information, the less enthusiastically it will be received, and the less likely it will be put to good use. There is one exception to this harsh reality—cold cases; any information which heats up a cold case always translates into "points on the board".

Irrespective of the situation and the motivational value of the information, a lengthy intelligence producing process is generally undesirable. **The longer it takes to identify the shooters (like habitually armed criminals, drug traffickers, and violent street gangs), the more opportunities they will have to shoot and perhaps maim or kill again.**

The acceptable amount of time that it should take to process this data and develop this type of intelligence should be determined not by the practitioners or bureaucrats but rather by the public they both serve.

When faced with a family grieving over the murder of a loved one, do any of the following statements communicate that justice will be served?

- "We'll get to this case when we can."

- "We are short of resources."

- "Our first priorities are shootings by police and cases going to trial."

Technologies exist today that are field proven and widely attainable. When adopted and adapted as necessary, they can provide sustainable ways to accelerate processes like national ballistic information database checks and overcome the unnecessary and bureaucratic process described in the city of New Haven scenario above.

A number of enlightened and locked-on law enforcement agencies have done just that. They've adopted new technology and adapted their procedures to include a new way of working that was made possible by the technology. For example, the West Palm Beach and Phoenix Police Departments have adopted the highly automated IBIS TRAX-3D technology which makes it possible for them to test fire a suspected crime gun within minutes or hours and electronically launch a search of the NIBIN database from their offices in the police department. The next day, the lab can determine if there is a probable match. From this point on, the process advances with confidence that time and resources are being well spent. The fact that the NIBIN data entry was performed outside the lab by the police means that the lab did not have to do it. The police department removed that burden from the lab's shoulders. The experts at the lab can then focus on what they do best—rendering their expert opinions. It is a win for the police in that they have significantly shortened a process that—at best—once took several weeks (or was never done at all) and reduced it to less than the time it takes to get a suit back from the cleaners.

There may be some who will try and find fault with this more efficient and effective process and it is their right to disagree. Their motives may range from being purely process-oriented to "protecting their turf"— sometimes it can be hard to tell. This is why **no one single stakeholder should be given the unquestionable authority and power to make such an important and wide reaching decision without the collaboration of the other stakeholders.** All affected stakeholders should collaborate on the development of a crime gun processing protocol. Stakeholders include, but are not limited to:

- Police

- Forensic personnel

- Prosecutors

Ballistic Information Sharing Networks

As business has become more global, so too has crime. Drug cartels are teaming up with organized street gangs to extend their reach and range. As drugs and other contraband move through channels which transcend international boundaries, guns and violence follow. There is a growing interest in sharing information about firearm related crime between countries—and the movement is well under way.

In the late 1990s, Denmark, Norway, and Sweden lay claim to the first international ballistic sharing initiative between the three countries. In fact, the world's very first international IBIS match was a product of that Scandinavian initiative.

In 2006, the United States and Canada also began sharing IBIS ballistic data between their respective national networks, NIBIN in the United

States and the Canadian Integrated Ballistics Identification Network (CIBIN) in Canada.

In May 2009, INTERPOL and Forensic Technology, the developer of IBIS, launched a new public-private partnership that allows INTERPOL to act as the world's first international hub for the cross-border exchange of ballistic data.

In an effort to give INTERPOL member countries access to essential investigative tools, INTERPOL is providing the network through which any INTERPOL member country that is equipped with IBIS will be able to share and compare ballistic data. This INTERPOL Ballistic Information Network (IBIN) is the only large-scale international ballistic data sharing network in the world.

In April 2009, President Obama announced, during a trip to Mexico, that among a number of joint initiatives to combat arms trafficking and violence between the United States and Mexico, these two countries would "bridge their IBIS systems in order to share digital images, ballistic markings, and other arms-related information to help identify leads in violent crimes both in Mexico and in the United States."

This agreement is now part of the United States National Southwest Border Counternarcotics Strategy issued by the White House Office of National Drug Control Policy.

Firearm Tracing Systems

IBIS® Firecycle™ is a Web-based firearm information management solution that can efficiently track the life cycle of a firearm, from manufacture, through various transactions and, ultimately, to final disposition or destruction. One of Firecycle's strengths is its integration with IBIS-generated ballistic data into a comprehensive firearm crime prevention and enforcement program. Because they are designed as compatible information technology solutions, Firecycle and IBIS can quickly and easily share data over communication networks and across multiple jurisdictions. Together, Firecycle and IBIS allow for a sustainable solution for improving and increasing the capacity to collect, maintain, and share critical firearm information.

eTrace[6] (Electronic Tracing System) is a Web-based system that allows participating law enforcement agencies to submit firearm traces on U.S. sourced firearms (e.g., U.S. manufactured or imported) to the ATF National Tracing Center (NTC). Authorized users can receive firearm trace results via this same Web site, search a database of all firearm traces submitted by their individual agency, and perform analytical functions.

Fingerprint Identification Systems

AFIS (Automated Fingerprint Identification System) is used in the process of automatically searching unknown fingerprints against a database of known and unknown prints. Automated fingerprint identification systems are primarily used by law enforcement agencies for criminal identification initiatives, the most important of which includes identifying a person suspected of committing a crime and linking a suspect to other unsolved crimes.

DNA Indexing Systems

CODIS[7] (Combined DNA Index System) is a software program that operates local, state, and national databases of DNA profiles from convicted offenders, unsolved crime scene evidence, and missing persons. Every state in the United States has a statutory provision for the establishment of a DNA database that allows for the collection of DNA profiles from offenders convicted of particular crimes. CODIS software enables all law enforcement crime laboratories to compare DNA profiles electronically, thereby linking serial crimes to each other and identifying suspects by matching DNA profiles from crime scenes with profiles from convicted offenders.

Overall, technology has been proven to be an indispensible crime fighting tool for law enforcement. Some technologies can be applied toward a broad category of crimes. For example, fingerprint and DNA technologies are applied to crimes involving anything from arson to zip guns, helping to link a particular person to a particular crime.

---

[6] www.atfonline.gov/etrace

[7] www.dna.gov

Automated ballistic identification technologies generally link a gun to a particular crime or series of crimes and link two or more crimes together by identifying that they were committed with the same firearm. Ballistics technologies can help police link crimes, guns, and suspects, and have been shown to be particularly effective in situations involving gang violence.

A Case Study: Stockton, California

In Stockton, California, Gang and Homicide investigators teamed up with their own ballistic imaging specialists, state prosecutors, and forensic experts to form a true crime-solving partnership targeting Cambodian Street Gangs.

Over a three year period, the partners relied on the NIBIN network and IBIS ballistic imaging technology to link evidence from 83 gang-related shootings and test fires from 35 seized firearms, two of which were machine guns.

From the IBIS links, police generated actionable intelligence leading to the execution of 55 search warrants and the arrest of 25 "gangsters" for six murders, 22 firearm assaults, and 50 drive-by shootings.

In the end, 16 criminals were convicted for crimes involving the murders and shootings. The criminals received lengthy prison sentences including life without parole as well as one death penalty verdict.

Networks such as NIBIN can share critical data quickly across multiple jurisdictions. These networks provide enormous strength and value because certain evidence that may seem insignificant to the agency that is entering the data can be the missing link that breaks open a case for an agency in a nearby jurisdiction. The more evidence that is entered into the system, the more crimes, guns, and suspects that will be linked, and the more information investigators will have to put violent criminals behind bars. The evidence of one can now be the evidence of all.

Recommended Best Practices

- Adopt and adapt to the technology available. Adopt what you need and adapt to its highest degree of usefulness and be prepared to adopt any new processes required to get to that level.

- Map the current processes that are in place for managing the information inside and outside the gun (e.g., firearm transaction record keeping, ballistic examination, fingerprints, DNA, hairs, and fibers) to identify the bottlenecks.

Key Considerations

- Understand where you are and where you want to go in terms of your current capabilities to collect and process the crime related and non-crime related information needed to exploit the information inside and outside the gun.

- Identify potential wide area networks for cross-jurisdictional and cross-discipline (e.g., ballistics, fingerprints, DNA, firearm transaction records) data processing and sharing.

Summary

The Most Important Thing: Adopting new crime fighting technologies and adapting to the change in processes required to maximize the technology's benefits of increased speed and productivity in order to identify armed criminals more quickly, before they have an opportunity to shoot and kill again.

The Next Step: While technology plays a key role in helping to sustain the presumptive approach, crime solving success is dependent on much more. The next chapter deals with the importance of balancing people, processes, and technology for sustained success crime solving success.

3

Chapter

People, Processes, and Technology

Murder is unique in that it abolishes the party it injures, so that society has to take the place of the victim and on his behalf demand atonement or grant forgiveness; it is the one crime in which society has a direct interest.

W. H. Auden critic & poet (1907–1973)

Why Do We Need All Three?

When one member of society harms another intentionally it is generally called a crime. Criminals must be held accountable by a society seeking peace and justice for all. So it is the people who have the responsibility to find the perpetrators, try them in a court of law and, if found guilty, prevent them from doing further harm.

People can become more efficient and effective in solving and preventing crime through the use of innovative processes and applied technology. Technology can help speed up and sustain processes and help make people more productive. However, technology is useless without people who can use it in an efficient manner.

A Case Study: Chicago, Illinois

September 30, 1995 (Chicago): A drive-by shooting occurred in which a 19-year-old man was killed and another was wounded. Fired cartridge cases were retained as evidence from the crime scene and entered into the NIBIN database using IBIS technology.

September 28, 2003: Police stopped a vehicle with a shattered rear window and seized a Glock pistol.

June 22, 2004: The crime lab used IBIS to search the test fires from the Glock pistol against the NIBIN database. The NIBIN query linked the test fires to the evidence from the earlier drive-by shooting. Police knew that they had the murder weapon in hand.

October 7, 2004: ATF traced the transaction history of the murder weapon to a woman who said that she bought the gun for her boyfriend named Coggs. Coggs was a felon and therefore unable to buy guns legally. She gave police the names of more witnesses.

May 17, 2005: Police interviewed one of those witnesses—he had been with Coggs when he killed the 19-year old during the drive-by shooting. The witness testified before a grand jury.

May 18, 2005: Coggs, a one-time enforcer for the "Gangster Disciples" street gang was arrested and charged with the murder.

This case highlights three critical points:

- It takes people, processes, and technology to adopt the presumptive approach.

- The ballistic data from inside the gun and the identifying data from outside the gun must be exploited.

- Information must be generated and acted upon in a timely fashion.

The Three-Legged Stool

Just as each leg of the three-legged stool depends on the other two to do its part to carry the load, a properly balanced combination of people, processes, and technology is needed to solve crime in today's society.

The Chicago case is an excellent example of "every crime gun has a story to tell". It also calls attention to the need for determining the right balance that must be applied to a given crime problem in order to develop timely solutions.

Finding the right combination of people, processes, and technology and applying it in a properly balanced manner requires a deliberate and collaborative effort on the part of all stakeholders (e.g., police, forensic, prosecutorial).

The temptation exists for some of the stakeholders to try and put programs in place which will work in favor of their own group's self interests. This is dangerous because it can stifle innovation, breakdown the spirit of collaboration between the stakeholders, and divert attention from crime-solving. The initiative to which the people, processes, and technology will be directed must have a well-aimed objective: **to provide timely and sustainable crime solving benefits to the public**. Placing public interest at the forefront of the discussion and decision-making process will shift the stakeholder's perspective from an internal focus to an external focus. An external focus will cause the stakeholder to think differently about potential solutions, rather than approaching the problems from their own internal perspectives. Impediments, such as inter-agency politics and "turf protection" tend to fade when the discussion is redirected externally to protecting the public. Allowing these obstacles and introspective intentions to upset the proper balance will eventually cause the three-legged stool to topple.

Recommended Best Practices

- *The 13 Critical Tasks Workshop* (provided by Forensic Technology) brings the principal criminal justice stakeholders together and leads them through a step-by-step collaborative process to generate consensus on ways that gun crime in their region can best be investigated and prevented. The workshop promotes the proper tactical and strategic utilization of important crime data so that it can be translated into actions by law enforcement that are derived from actionable intelligence. The workshop also introduces the stakeholders to a number of well-established best practices which have been proven to help others better address their gun crime problems. Most importantly, the workshop provides a facilitated forum for the stakeholders to develop a sustainable gun violence reduction program which balances the people, processes, and technology so as to serve the best interests of the public.

Key Considerations

- People: Identify the stakeholders and think and act together as group to design a well-balanced comprehensive solution that can be institutionalized.

- Processes: Ensure that all of the information available on the inside and outside of gun is collected and exploited for crime-solving purposes, as part of the standard operating procedure (SOP) for investigating crimes committed with firearms. The SOP must become institutionalized—up, down, and across the affected stakeholder organizations.

- Technology: Adopt and adapt to technology with the purpose of providing stakeholders with the tools they need to help them be more efficient and effective in their work.

- People, processes and technology: Balance all three in a manner which will provide maximum crime-solving benefits to the public.

Summary

The Most Important Thing: Understanding the fact that balancing people, processes, and technology is not only an objective but is also a means of overcoming obstacles and bridging gaps to achieve the goal which is to provide sustainable and substantial crime solving benefits to the public we all serve.

The Next Step: The desire for the achievement of sustainable benefits for the public is what drove the development of *The 13 Critical Tasks*. The next chapter details the reasoning that went into the development of this project and the outcome of those efforts.

4
Chapter

The Development of the 13 Critical Tasks

Why Were They Developed?

Forensic Technology provides solutions that assist law enforcement agencies around the world in their efforts to reduce violent crime. As a solutions provider, Forensic Technology has seen some agencies stand out as highly successful users of IBIS, while others do not. These "power users" share many things in common in terms of the critical tasks they perform in order to sustain their successes.

How Were They Developed?

In May 2005, in an effort to see as many customers as possible achieve the maximum benefits from their IBIS investment, Forensic Technology began an aggressive project to identify the tasks that are critical to operating an efficient and effective ballistic information sharing network. A core working group was formed; it consisted of experienced IBIS power users, members of the academic community, and Forensic Technology personnel who were experienced in forensic ballistics, firearm crime investigation, and the IBIS technology.

The core working group contributed best practices by drawing upon their personal experiences with IBIS or by reporting on observations they had made during visits to other IBIS power users around the world. The core group also searched for commonalities in the ways in which power users integrated ballistics technology into their crime solving processes.

All of this information was used by the core working group to answer one very carefully crafted question: **"What critical tasks must be performed to operate an efficient and effective integrated ballistic information network program that provides substantial and sustainable crime solving benefits to the public?"**

A great deal of care went into drafting the question because the quality and accuracy of the answers received are often dependent on the content of the question itself. With the specific intent to expand the group's thinking well beyond the forensic discipline of firearm examination and the IBIS technology, the question was revised and tweaked numerous times. Key words like: efficient, effective, integrated, program, substantial, sustainable, crime solving, benefits, and public were inserted after much discussion and with deliberate meaning attached.

The Results

As a result, *The 13 Critical Tasks* were developed. They form the basis for a complete firearm crime-solving program, *The 13 Critical Tasks Workshop*, which goes beyond just being a set of best practices for using ballistics technology. This book and *The 13 Critical Tasks Workshop* delve deeply into the tasks that must be addressed when establishing sustainable protocols and ways in which to balance the people, processes, and technology. Protocols are needed in order to collect and analyze all of the available data that can be obtained from crime guns and related evidence for crime solving and crime prevention purposes.

These commonsense steps can be used to help identify and establish a series of consistently applied protocols to ensure that all of the valuable information from inside and outside of a crime gun is exploited by police and forensic agencies in a given region so as to generate leads to stop armed criminals before they can do more harm.

The 13 Critical Tasks

- Managing Stakeholders

- Integrating Programs

- Establishing a Formal Understanding and Reinforcing Directives

- Collecting Firearm and Related Evidence

- Transferring Evidence

- Assessing and Evaluating Evidence

- Test-firing

- Acquiring Images of Fired Ammunition Components

- Reviewing Correlation Results

- Confirming Hits

- Communicating Hit Information

- Leveraging Tactics and Strategies

- Improving Programs

Asking the Right Question

Crime solving benefits and *public*: These words identified satisfying the public as the ultimate objective. With this goal in mind, the core working group looked at improvements in firearm crime-solving from the public's point of view, instead of that of the police or the forensic labs. The public isn't interested in agency rivalries, feuds, and excuses like "that's their job not ours" or "that's our job not theirs". The public wants law enforcement agencies to use common sense and good judgment. Therefore, during the core working group's discussions, the interests of the public were always at the forefront and served as a standard to be met. The personnel, processes, and technology employed by the police, the forensic lab, and the prosecuting attorney were certainly a major focus of the core working group's analysis, albeit from the external and service-oriented perspective when determining how resources could be best used to provide sustainable crime solving benefits to the public.

If you are still not convinced, then try replacing the word "public" with "police", "forensic lab" or "prosecuting attorney" at the end of the carefully-crafted driving question and see what answers come to mind.

Efficient and *effective*: These words were intended to ensure that, in terms of people, processes, and technology, the invested time and effort were worth the resulting rewards.

Integrated and *program*: These words were intended to ensure that informational and institutional bottlenecks that interfere with crime solving success were eliminated up, down, and across the affected stakeholder organizations and that programs of action would be created so that they would be well defined, adequately funded, and measured for efficiency and effectiveness.

Substantial and *sustainable*: These words were intended to ensure that the benefits delivered would be considerable, not inconsequential. The levels of people, processes, and technology required for success must be able to be maintained for as long as required. Successful crime reduction programs and processes must be institutionalized so that they may instinctively be recognized as the proper way of doing things.

Summary

The Most Important Thing: Following *The 13 Critical Tasks* developed by law enforcement and forensic practitioners in consultation with renowned academic researchers to integrate and leverage tactics and strategies to provide substantial and sustainable firearm crime-solving benefits to the public in an efficient and effective manner.

The Next Step: The next chapter discusses the fundamentals of task number one of *The 13 Critical Tasks*—Managing Stakeholders.

5 Chapter

Task One: Managing Stakeholders

Why Do We Need to Manage Stakeholders?

The reduction of violent crime is a complex problem and the task is too large and difficult for one lab, police department or prosecutor to manage alone. Only the right combination of stakeholders can plan and implement the improvements needed to reduce violent crime. Yet, the involvement of more stakeholders results in more diverse perspectives, which translates into more issues and requirements that need to be addressed. Success often depends on the ability to address a problem from a variety of fronts. All of the right people involved must be thinking and acting together—not only at the outset, but throughout the entire process. Plain old cooperation will not be enough to drive stakeholder management—a stronger action is required. The level of action needed is best described by the word **collaboration**. It becomes a fundamental driver for securing a sustainable solution capable of delivering substantial benefits.

Taking the presumptive approach to the efficient and effective investigation of gun crime begins by assembling the right groups of people and getting them to think and act together.

Forming Groups

In order to assemble groups, there must be an influential senior level policy advocate or advocates to champion the concept. The champions must have the clout needed to bring the various stakeholders together in an effective spirit of collaboration and partnership.

Champions can be bred along the way as part of the stakeholder management process—step one of *The 13 Critical Tasks*. One way of doing this is to convene two groups of key stakeholders.

Strategic Group

The first group of stakeholders is policy oriented and should be made up of key senior managers and policy makers representing, at a minimum, three broad criminal justice perspectives: police, forensic, and prosecutorial. It is from this first group that the champions of the presumptive approach should emerge. This group should be kept as small as possible yet should represent the major police, forensic, and prosecutorial organizations at the local, county, and state levels serving the targeted affected crime region[8]. Representatives from certain federal agencies must also be included in this group (e.g., in the U.S., ATF and the U.S. Attorney's Office). This group must be strategically oriented and empowered to create vision, mandate new policy, provide direction, and request resources. This group can produce multiple champions.

For example, Massachusetts had several champions representing major city police organizations (the Boston Police Department, the state police and forensic labs), the Department of Public Safety, ATF, and the state and federal prosecutor's offices. This small group of champions had the influence and leadership required in order to drive law enforcement policy for the entire Commonwealth of Massachusetts.

Tactical Group

The second group of stakeholders is operation oriented and should be made up of mid-level managers, first line supervisors, and line practitioners from the various interdependent units within the police, forensic, and prosecutorial services which have a role to play in taking the presumptive approach to the investigation of crimes involving the misuse of firearms. This second group should also consist of representatives of organizations at the local, county, state, and federal levels that serve the targeted affected crime region. This second group must be tactically oriented and must represent the various interdependent subgroups charged with enforcing the law and supporting the judicial process (e.g., patrol, investigations, special units, forensics, and prosecutors). The members of this tactically oriented group are experts at what they do. They know what is working well and what needs to be improved. They

---

[8] The affected crime region is a geographic area in which criminals are most likely to be crisscrossing police jurisdictions in the course of their criminal activities (e.g., gang activity and drug trafficking).

can quickly identify their people-, process-, and technology-related needs as well as the obstacles blocking their way and the gaps they must bridge.

Two very different examples of the importance of influential champions to the formation of these working groups come to mind.

In the first example, a simple form letter to a mayor whose city was in the process of coming to grips with increasing levels of gang- and gun-related crime, trickled down through the Police Chief to the Commander of Investigations. Instead of pushing back, the Commander kept an open mind and—while powered by the inertia created by the mayor's referral— seized upon an opportunity to bring the various stakeholders together to discuss gun crime protocols. This effort went on to develop a very successful program which is the subject of a case study in the final chapters of this book.

The other example is one in which key law enforcement stakeholders were brought together by senior state and federal officials to discuss the merits of a statewide crime gun processing protocol. One key stakeholder was immediately averse to the prospect. This was problematic because the stakeholder's lab provided forensic services for most of the police agencies in the state. The stakeholder was concerned that more work would simply be dumped on them without regard for their capacity to respond, so he pushed back. The influential government leaders in the room assured the stakeholder that no new workloads would be imposed unless he was balanced in terms of people, processes, and technology. The stakeholder left the meeting unconvinced. A second meeting was held about two months later. This time, the recalcitrant stakeholder reported that over the intervening period between the two meetings, it was noticed that more evidence was being received and more hits were being made. The stakeholder attributed this to the common-sense messages delivered at the first meeting about the value of regional crime gun protocols. The stakeholder said "it's working already". From that point on, the stakeholder who had been pushing back took the lead, asserted rightful ownership of the project, and moved it forward.

Meetings

A series of meetings with each working group should be conducted by experienced facilitators and structured to efficiently manage the attendees' time. The meetings should surface relevant issues, identify obstacles and gaps, and ensure sustainability of the solutions that are formulated by identifying the proper balance of people, processes, and technology. The meetings should also identify how the presumptive approach will be employed and how success will be measured. This includes how the tactical and strategic information needed for crime solving and crime prevention is developed, processed, and shared in a timely and sustainable manner.

Collaboration becomes the key component for developing a sustainable crime solving and crime prevention program based on the presumptive approach.

The strategic group should meet first in a relatively short facilitated session (i.e., no more than two or three hours) designed to provide an overview of the many issues and handoffs involved in using the presumptive approach when investigating gun crimes. The goal of this policy maker's session is to generate high level commitment to enlist the people, processes, and technology required for the presumptive approach.

Once the strategic policy makers commit to moving forward and champions emerge, the onus then shifts to the tactically oriented group.

The tactical group should meet in a one- or two- day facilitated session. The meeting should begin by presenting the same information that was presented to the strategically oriented group of senior policy makers, laying out the issues and handoffs required in taking the presumptive approach. This group must then delve more deeply into the various issues. It must formulate recommendations regarding the people, processes, and technology that will be required and then forward the recommendations to the strategic policy makers for approval, resource fulfillment, and promulgation.

The 13 Critical Tasks Workshop **was designed to facilitate this meeting process and provide the in-depth analysis required for the development of a program based on the presumptive approach for dealing with gun crime.**

Assuming that such a program is recommended and authorized, the requirement for effective stakeholder management continues as an essential element of program implementation. **Therefore, a process for continued stakeholder management for both the strategic (policy) and tactical (operations) working groups will be critical to**

developing and, more importantly, to sustaining the collaborative partnership.

Recommended Best Practices

New York "COMPSTAT"

In 1994, William Bratton, who was then Commissioner of the New York City Police Department, implemented a crime control model called COMPSTAT (Computer Statistics) to allow maximum intelligence sharing based on four tenets: accurate and timely intelligence, effective tactics, rapid deployment, and relentless follow-up and assessment. Years later, Bratton would become Chief of the Los Angeles Police Department where he implemented the COMPSTAT model for the tactical and strategic deployment of resources to fight crime.

Below is a brief of Chief Bratton's COMPSTAT[9] model:

> Accurate & Timely Intelligence: COMPSTAT eliminates the traditional barriers among the various organizational units through weekly meetings designed to bring the affected units together to review the computer data and discuss ways to combat crime in specific places. The meetings serve as a forum in which precinct and other operational unit commanders communicate the problems they face to the agency's top executives, while also sharing successful crime reduction tactics with other commanders. Since today's policing techniques nearly always consist of vast amounts of information, it is necessary to provide a vehicle wherein essential information can easily and effectively be shared with all levels of the organization.
>
> Effective Tactics: COMPSTAT tactics encourage "thinking outside the box" and mandates that every resource, both internal and external, is considered in responding to a problem. On a weekly basis, police compile a statistical summary of the week's crime complaint, arrest and summons activity, as well as a written recapitulation of significant cases, crime patterns, and police

---

[9] www.lapdonline.org/crime_maps_and_compstat/content_basic_view/6363

activities. COMPSTAT tactics also provide for a sense of urgency in responding to problems.

Rapid Deployment: Every case (e.g., shooting incident) is thoroughly and rapidly investigated in a systematic manner. With COMPSTAT, the police make use of vital intelligence regarding emerging crime trends or patterns that allows for a rapid strategic police response. The strategic response can be in many forms, both traditional and non-traditional operations.

Relentless Follow-up and Assessment: Follow-up and assessment of results are an essential part of the process. Data is presented on a week-to-date, prior 30 days, and year-to-date basis, with comparisons to previous years' activity. Precinct commanders and members of the agency's top management can easily discern emerging and established crime trends, as well as deviations and anomalies, and can easily make comparisons between commands.

In applying the COMPSTAT model to the presumptive approach discussed in this book, the collaborative planning discussions and the effective sharing of information must also extend beyond the local police organization to include the forensic and prosecutorial stakeholders, and other local, state and federal partners as well.

Project Safe Neighborhoods (PSN)

Project Safe Neighborhoods, a program that is administered by the United States Department of Justice (DOJ), is an outstanding example of a pyramid of champions that is focused on reducing gun and gang violence by collaborative stakeholder planning and execution, leveraging and integrating programs, communication and outreach, and personal accountability.

PSN also adds another very important element that is critical for success—**the resources to help get the job done.** PSN helps provide the participating stakeholders with the tools they need in terms of people, processes, and technology.

The following information can be found on the Project Safe Neighborhoods Web site: www.psn.gov

PSN is a nationwide commitment to reduce gun and gang crime in America by networking existing local programs that target gun and gun crime and providing these programs with additional tools necessary to be successful. Since its inception in 2001, approximately $2 billion has been committed to this initiative. This funding is being used to hire new federal and state prosecutors, support investigators, provide training, distribute gun lock safety kits, deter juvenile gun crime, and develop and promote community outreach efforts as well as to support other gun and gang violence reduction strategies.

PSN is based on three fundamental principles, specifically it is:

Comprehensive: While enforcement is a necessary and important aspect of crime reduction programs, the most successful initiatives marry enforcement with prevention and deterrence efforts.

Coordinated: Programs that ensure coordination between the enforcement, deterrence and prevention efforts are more likely to succeed than those that do not.

Community-based: Gun crime is local, and the resources available to address it vary from district to district. Accordingly, any national gun crime reduction program must remain sufficiently flexible for jurisdictions to implement it in a way that both responds to the specific problem in that area, and accounts for the particular local capacities and resources that can be dedicated to it.

National Integrated Ballistic Information Network (NIBIN)

NIBIN is the world's first national ballistic information sharing network that is capable of processing both fired bullets and cartridge cases on a single platform. Within the ballistic network context, NIBIN is a best practice model for stakeholder management.

The following information can be found on the ATF NIBIN Web site: www.nibin.gov

Purpose: In 1999, ATF established and began administration of the National Integrated Ballistic Information Network (NIBIN). In this program, ATF administers automated ballistic imaging technology for NIBIN Partners: Federal, State and local law enforcement agencies. NIBIN allows NIBIN Partners to acquire (enter) digital images of the markings made on spent ammunition recovered from a crime scene or a crime gun test fire. The images are then correlated (in a matter of hours) against earlier entries via electronic image comparison. If a high-confidence candidate for a match emerges, the original evidence is compared via microscope to confirm the match or NIBIN "hit." By searching in an automated environment either locally, regionally, or nationally, NIBIN Partners are able to discover links between crimes more quickly, including links that would never have been identified absent the technology. NIBIN also makes it easier to search investigative information across jurisdictional boundaries.

Goals: Coordinate the comprehensive NIBIN entry of all ballistic information (suitable for NIBIN entry) taken into Federal, State, and local law enforcement custody in order to identify all possible links to violent shootings.

o   Refer NIBIN-generated investigative leads to NIBIN Participants in order to solve, reduce, and prevent firearms-related violent crimes

o   Record the investigative/prosecutorial results of NIBIN-generated investigative leads in order to measure performance

o   Provide the best NIBIN "best practices" training for all NIBIN participants.

o   Provide the best NIBIN user training for all NIBIN Partners.

o   Provide the best NIBIN technology for all NIBIN Partners.

NIBIN Partners: NIBIN Partners must enter into an agreement with ATF to use the equipment to a reasonable degree, share hit information with other NIBIN participants, enter as much ballistic information from shooting scenes as possible, provide adequate staffing to operate the equipment, fund new user travel for a one-week training course, possess a casing/bullet recovery system for firearms test firing, and employ or have access to a certified firearm examiner to complete microscopic comparisons. NIBIN connects over 200 IBIS systems at almost 200 locations.

NIBIN Executive Board: ATF oversees a NIBIN Executive Board comprised of Federal, State, and local law enforcement representation that recommends and provides guidance to ATF regarding NIBIN operations; rules, regulations, and procedures; ballistic imaging technology, standards, applications, and networking; contract matters, procurements and expenditures; software and hardware upgrades; and deployments, moves, and removals.

National Ballistic Intelligence Service (NABIS)

NABIS is a program that is administered by the Home Office[10] in the United Kingdom which grew out of a textbook case involving championship, stakeholder management and collaboration, and program integration. It began with several key presumptive-approach champions. Their efforts led to an initial program of work commissioned by the Home Office and Association of Chief Police Officers (ACPO) to cover the 43 police forces in England and Wales[11]. This effort concentrated on the development of a collaborative understanding among all of the stakeholders of the various inputs, outputs, and outcomes involved in such a crime gun program.

The initial program of action resulted in the establishment of NABIS to ensure that law enforcement in the United Kingdom had an efficient and effective means of sharing ballistic information and intelligence about the criminal misuse of firearms.

The following information can be found on the NABIS Web site at: www.nabis.police.uk

> NABIS provides an intelligence resource that is available to police forces and other law enforcement agencies that focuses entirely on the criminal use of firearms. It comprises three separate but interlinked elements, namely:

---

[10] The Home Office is the lead government department in the United Kingdom for immigration and passports, drug policy, counter-terrorism and police.

[11] Work is already underway to fully incorporate the Scottish police forces into NABIS.

o   A complete registry of all recovered firearms and ammunition coming into police possession in England and Wales

o   A ballistics comparison capability to link crimes and incidents within 24 to 48 hours in urgent cases

o   An associated intelligence database to provide strategic and tactical intelligence capable of focusing law enforcement activity

NABIS relies on a national database for all recovered firearms and ballistic material, such as complete rounds of ammunition, cartridge cases, and projectiles. The database also links those ballistic items to tactical intelligence recorded by police forces and other UK law enforcement agencies.

NABIS is made up of police officers and police staff. Some team members are employed directly by the Service and others are seconded from police forces.

Three new NABIS regional facilities will test fire, analyze and link firearms and materials to other incidents across the UK. This gives investigating officers access to the quick time intelligence essential within an investigation. The facilities will use the latest equipment and will be at the forefront of firearms forensic technology.

NABIS is funded by a subscription-based arrangement agreed by from the ACPO.

Critical Elements

- Develop a senior level champion who has enough influence to drive the initiative to bring all the right people into the process.

- Identify and assign participants for the strategic (policy) and tactical (operations) stakeholder groups.

- Conduct a facilitated presumptive approach awareness session for the strategic stakeholder working group to generate a broader consortium of champions.

- Conduct a facilitated presumptive approach protocol development workshop for the tactical stakeholder working group and transmit recommendations to the strategic group.

- Plan to integrate existing programs for leveraging the presumptive approach.

- Plan, develop, and implement a sustainable regional program to quickly generate crime solving and crime prevention benefits by taking the presumptive approach to the investigation of crimes involving the misuse of firearms.

- Be prepared to communicate the new program protocols and expectations to all affected stakeholders.

- Establish an ongoing process of performance monitoring between the two working groups to ensure that the initiative is well coordinated and is achieving the intended objectives.

- Communicate clearly and often.

Key Considerations

- Assemble the right teams of people and sustained collaborative interaction.

- Clarify each stakeholder's input and output needs.

- Map the stakeholder's current processes to identify existing bottlenecks and gaps.

- Avoid bottlenecks that prevent collaboration.

- Create new and sustainable protocols that are balanced in terms of people, processes, and technology.

- Employ a continuous communication process with affected stakeholders—up, down, and across their various organizations.

- Validate the sustainability of successes through program reviews and corrective actions.

- Institutionalize the new protocols within the affected organizations.

Summary

The Most Important Thing: Developing a champion or champions that have the power to drive change at the required levels to assemble the various stakeholders needed for taking the presumptive approach and to provide or advocate for resource support for the people, processes, and technology tools that will be needed.

The Next Step: In a manner that is analogous to the way in which bridge cables are constructed, integration and leveraging can help provide crime solving programs with the sustainable strength needed to deliver substantial public safety benefits. The next chapter discusses the fundamentals of task number two of *The 13 Critical Tasks*—Integrating Programs.

6
Chapter

Task Two: Integrating Programs

Why Do We Need to Integrate Programs?

Look around the law enforcement community and you will find many ingenious crime reducing programs. Some agencies have dozens of programs that correctly approach the crime problem from various perspectives.

For example, Project Exile is a program that focuses on career criminals whose unlawful possession of firearms exposed them to lengthy minimum mandatory prison sentences effectively removing them from the communities that they preyed upon.

Also, the Boston Gun Project—Operation Ceasefire is a problem-oriented policing initiative aimed at homicides committed by young people in Boston. Stakeholders were brought together from law enforcement, the community, and academia to help find solutions.

Anti-crime programs viewed as individual "silos" and executed within organizational "stovepipes" are, overall, less efficient and less effective at solving crime. They waste time and resources and, by their nature, cause important information to fall through the gaps. They are simply not as strong as they could be.

Effective crime fighting improvements must have the strength needed to sustain the delivery of expected benefits over long periods of time. Crime solving improvements that cannot be sustained are not improvements at all and can actually have the opposite effect, especially in terms damage to the public's trust and confidence in government.

The Steel Cables

Consider the following analogy. Suspension bridges carry heavy loads and need great strength which comes in large part from the massive cables that support them. The construction of a bridge cable can provide a lesson for leveraging the power of programs through integration. Each cable gets its strength from the integration of many individual filaments of steel wire. The strength of each individual filament of wire is leveraged by weaving them together into steel "ropes". The much stronger ropes are then leveraged in the same way to form a cable. This escalating continuum of integration not only gives the bridge cable the strength it needs to sustain its load but the fabrication methodology itself provides an efficient and effective way to build the bridge.

Much in the same way that bridge cables are constructed, integration and leveraging can help provide crime solving programs with the sustainable strength needed to deliver substantial public safety benefits. For example, consider this fairly typical scenario. Law enforcement agency "X" has three firearm crime-related programs in operation: (1) NIBIN for linking guns to crimes, (2) eTrace[12] for linking people to guns, and (3) crime mapping software for plotting the locations of "calls for service" incidents. Each program is run by a different unit of the organization, separated by function and supervision. NIBIN is situated under the Forensic Services Unit, eTrace under the Investigative Services Unit, and crime mapping under the Planning and Research Unit. The three programs are, for the most part, silos functioning and providing information within each one's own domain. For example, in the Forensic Services Unit, crime guns and ballistic evidence are being processed through NIBIN. The fired bullets and cartridge cases found at crime scenes are being linked to each other and to the guns that fired them. In the Investigative Services Unit, crime guns taken into police custody are being traced through eTrace. Detectives are learning the names of the people who purchased them and are pursuing that information. The crime mapping efforts that are ongoing in the Planning and Research Unit are

---

[12]eTrace (Electronic Tracing System) is an Internet-based system that allows participating law enforcement agencies to submit firearm traces to the ATF National Tracing Center (NTC). Authorized users can receive firearm trace results via this same Internet Web site, search a database of all firearm traces submitted by their individual agency, and perform analytical functions.

helping the senior command staff visualize the hot spots needing attention in the city.

Now, picture the same scenario but with two significant changes:

First: assume that the three units involved are co-stakeholders operating in a manner structured to ensure collaboration as noted in chapter 5, "Task One: Managing Stakeholders".

Second: assume that they have taken the steps required to integrate and leverage the information from their three independently executed programs, as recommended in this chapter.

With these two changes in play, the **eTrace data** containing crime gun descriptions and the names and addresses of purchasers and sellers, and the **NIBIN data** with its crime gun and ammunition descriptions and identified links to crimes **are all being plotted on the crime map** along with other data from all shooting incidents, assaults, and murders. Now the police operations and administrative staff can visualize much more comprehensive firearm crime data; it is laid out before them in one place. They can quickly and easily begin to extract valuable information regarding the relationships between crimes, people, places, guns, and fired ammunition. Just as important as making the readily identifiable connections, is the ability to quickly spot the questionable gaps which, in turn, prompt further inquiry.

Just as in the bridge cable analogy, the three individual programs above make a much stronger gun violence reduction initiative when integrated and woven together. Program integration becomes a prerequisite for taking the presumptive approach because of the amount of information and the diverse nature of the firearm related information that must be collected and processed.

Recommended Best Practices

Project Safe Neighborhoods (PSN)

PSN is mentioned again here in this chapter "Program Integration" because of its relevance and effectiveness at leveraging diverse strengths and coordination up, down, and across multiple jurisdictions.

The following information can be found on the Project Safe Neighborhoods Web site: www.psn.gov

> The Department of Justice required that each United States Attorney implement a local gun crime reduction effort that contained each of the following five elements: **partnerships, strategic planning, training, outreach, and accountability.** The partnership element requires that the local U.S. Attorney create workable and sustainable partnerships with other federal, state, and local law enforcement; prosecutors; and the community. Strategic problem-solving involves the use of data and research to isolate the key factors driving gun crime at the local level, suggest intervention strategies, and provide feedback and evaluation to the task force. The outreach component incorporates communication strategies geared at both offenders ("focused deterrence") and the community ("general deterrence"). The training element underscores the importance of ensuring that each person involved in the gun crime reduction effort—from the line police officer to the prosecutor to the community outreach worker—has the skills necessary to be most effective. Finally, the accountability element ensures that the task force regularly receives feedback about the impact of its interventions so that adjustments can be made if necessary. A more detailed account of each element follows:

> *Partnerships:* The PSN program is intended to increase partnerships between federal, state, and local agencies through the formation of a local PSN task force. Coordinated by the U.S. Attorney's Office, the PSN task force typically includes both federal and local prosecutors, federal law enforcement agencies, local and state law enforcement agencies, and probation and parole. Nearly all PSN task forces also include additional members, such as representatives of local governments, social service providers, neighborhood leaders, members of the faith community, business leaders, educators, and health care providers.

> In addition to the local partnerships developed in each district, the national PSN program also adopted two national partners: the National District Attorneys Association and the International Association of Chiefs of Police. Although the national partners do not have a defined role, these groups have been integral in communicating – to their constituents, Congress, and others –

the importance of the initiative and need for continued support each budget cycle.

Strategic Planning: Recognizing that crime problems, including gun crime, vary from community to community across the United States, that state laws addressing gun crime vary considerably, and that local and state resources vary across the federal judicial districts covered by U.S. Attorneys' Offices, PSN also includes a commitment to tailor the program to local context. Specifically, PSN provided resources for the inclusion of a local research partner who worked with the PSN task force to analyze the local gun crime problem and help develop a proactive plan for gun crime reduction. The goal was for the research partners to assist the task force through analysis of gun crime patterns and trends that could help the task force focus resources on the most serious people, places, and contexts of gun violence. The research partners could also bring evidence-based practice to the task force discussions of gun crime reduction strategies. The inclusion of the research partner was also intended to assist in ongoing assessment in order to provide feedback to the task force. (See *Accountability* component, below.)

Although each district creates strategic interventions that make sense in its local context, one strategy shared by all PSN task forces is increased federal prosecution of gun crime. PSN is built on the belief that the increased federal prosecution of gun offenders will reduce gun crime through the incapacitation of gun criminals and the deterrence of potential offenders. This working hypothesis is based on the notion that federal sanctions for gun crime are often more severe than those either available at the state level or likely to be imposed at the state level. Further, federal prosecution may include sanctions unavailable at the local level. The focus on prohibited persons possessing or using a firearm is built on the finding that a significant portion of gun crime involves offenders with significant criminal histories. Thus, by increasing the certainty that a prohibited person in possession will face strong federal sanctions, the goal is to persuade potential offenders not to illegally possess and carry a gun.

Training: PSN has involved a significant commitment of resources to support training. This program has included training provided to law enforcement agencies on topics including gun crime investigations, crime gun identification and tracing, and related issues. Training on effective prosecution of gun cases has been provided to state and local prosecutors. Additional training has focused on strategic problem-solving and community outreach and engagement. Nationally-supported PSN training programs are hosted by a network of national training and technical assistance providers; in addition, local training sessions are conducted by each United States Attorney's Office.

Outreach: The architects of PSN believed that increased sanctions would have the most impact if accompanied with a media campaign to communicate the message of the likelihood of federal prosecution for illegal possession and use of a gun. Consequently, resources were provided to all PSN task forces to work with an outreach partner to devise strategies for communicating this message to both potential offenders and to the community at large. This local outreach effort is also supported at the national level by the creation and distribution of Public Service Announcements and materials (ads, posters). These materials are direct mailed to media outlets and are also available to local PSN task forces.

The outreach component is also intended to support the development of prevention and intervention components. PSN provided grant funding in fiscal years 2003 and 2004 to the local PSN partnerships that could be used to support a variety of initiatives including prevention and intervention. Many initiatives were built on existing programs such as school-based prevention, Weed and Seed, or juvenile court intervention programs.

Accountability: This element emphasized that PSN would focus on outcomes—i.e., reduced gun crime—as opposed to a focus on outputs such as arrests and cases prosecuted. That is, PSN's success is measured by the reduction in gun crime. This accountability component was linked to strategic planning whereby PSN task forces, working with their local research partner, are asked to monitor levels of crime over time within targeted problems and/or targeted areas.

To implement the program, each United States Attorney's Office has designated a PSN Coordinator who is responsible for the day-to-day operation of the initiative. The Department monitors the progress of the initiative through reports submitted by each United States Attorney. In addition, the Department established a point-of-contact for each district to assist with implementation issues and created the Firearms Enforcement Assistance Team (FEAT) to support the program overall. To help ensure that each district developed the skills it needed to implement the initiative, OJP has funded a comprehensive network of training and technical assistance providers, and hosts a PSN National Conference approximately every 18 months. Individual districts also have received grant funding, through a local fiscal agent, for each year of the program.

Violent Crime Impact Teams (VCIT)

Conceived by ATF, the VCIT strategy dictates applying technology to identify hot spots and to target, investigate, and arrest violent offenders. ATF's National Tracing Center, Crime Gun Analysis Branch, Regional Crime Gun Centers (RCGC), and other technologies, such as NIBIN and geographic information systems, are used to pinpoint localized crime problems and to identify the "worst of the worst" criminals. Integrating intelligence from local law enforcement agencies with information produced through new technologies is fundamental to successfully combating violent firearm crime.

Boston's Impact Players and Street Shootings Review

In the mid-1990s, the Boston Police Department implemented an initiative called the Boston Gun Project: Operation Ceasefire, upon which many of the tenets of Project Safe Neighborhoods (PSN) were built. It was based on collaborative partnerships, the integration of data from the programs of various law enforcement and criminal justice agencies, and the leveraging of grassroots organizations and the faith community. A key tactic of that project that continues in operation today the: Impact Players and Street Shootings Review (IPSSR).

The IPSSR brings together local and state police, prosecutors, and other federal and local agencies every two weeks to share intelligence on the "impact players" involved in drug- and gang-related violence in the city's designated hot spots. IBIS/NIBIN data and firearm trace data are two examples of the important information on which the IPSSR relies.

All information is managed through a central Tactical Intelligence Center that serves as the Boston Regional Intelligence Center (BRIC).

In addition to generating traditional investigative leads, the IPSSR also makes use of suppression tactics, such as imposing costs on offenders related to their chronic offending behavior (e.g., serving warrants, enforcing probation restrictions, deploying federal enforcement powers, and mandatory sentences). The IPSSR has many things in common with COMPSTAT and, as such, has been integrated as an element of the Boston PD COMPSTAT Program. Yet the IPSSR is also unique in that it fosters inter-organizational stakeholder collaboration focused on gang related firearm violence.

A Case Study: Cardoza's Cartridge

As part of the Boston Gun Project: Operation Ceasefire[13], various stakeholders from local, state, and federal law enforcement and the civilian sector were brought together in a formal and routine manner in order to collaborate on solutions to address the rising levels of gang violence on Boston's streets. The power of the various stakeholders meeting regularly to address a problem not only from their unique perspectives but by thinking and acting together as one is well exemplified in the story of Freddie Cardoza—a man who at one time was regarded by many in Boston's law enforcement community as one of the city's most heinous gang members.

*In the mid-1990s the participants at one of the Boston Operation Ceasefire meetings (the forerunner of IPSSR/COMPSTAT) were briefed on an incident in which Boston patrol officers found Cardoza in possession of a single round of ammunition—**one cartridge***.

In discussing the incident at the IPSSR meeting, the various stakeholders learned that by possessing a single cartridge, Cardoza had in fact violated the Federal Firearms laws and would qualify for enhanced mandatory sentencing because of his previous convictions for three or more violent crimes. The group called upon their ATF and U.S. Attorney colleagues to prosecute Cardoza for possession of the single cartridge. Cardoza was prosecuted and convicted. He was sentenced under the armed career criminal enhanced sentencing provision for gun and ammunition possession to a mandatory term of almost 20 years in Federal prison.

---

[13] Research Report: *Reducing Gun Violence – The Boston Gun Project's Operation Ceasefire*, September 2001, NCJ 188741

Despite the fact that a repeat violent offender had been removed from the community for a very long time, the stakeholders believed that more public benefits could and should be gained. They felt strongly that the no-tolerance stance which they had taken on Cardoza should be used as a tactic to deter other young people from committing acts of gang violence.

The working group developed a multi-prong strategy to "send a message" to would-be 'gangsters' that violence would not be tolerated in Boston. Posters, like the one below, were created and displayed throughout the city in areas where gangs frequently operated. Gang members were also brought in to face a panel of Operation Ceasefire stakeholders and hear firsthand just what the police and the courts had in store for armed gang members. Below is an excerpt from the Operation Ceasefire report:

. . . The room became more silent when the panel turned to Freddie Cardoza, who was featured on his own poster and handout. "One bullet," [said Gary French]. "We are not putting up with this stuff anymore." . . .

FREDDY CARDOZA

PROBLEM: VIOLENT GANG MEMBER

"Given his extensive criminal record,
if there was a Federal law against
jaywalking we'd indict him for that."
--Don Stern, US attorney

SOLUTION: ARMED CAREER
CRIMINCAL CONVICTION

Arrested with one bullet
Sentence: 19 years, 7 months
No possibility of parole

ADDRESS:

OTTISVILLE FEDERAL
CORRECTIONAL INSTITUTE
Maximum Security Facility, New York

Critical Elements

- Integrate information from the relevant crime programs (e.g., organized anti-gang initiatives, crime gun tracing, geo-crime mapping, and gunshot acoustic detectors) including forensic data such as ballistics, DNA, and fingerprints.

- Leverage inputs, outputs, and outcomes of relevant crime programs.

- Effectively process program output data for both tactical and strategic uses.

- Eliminate silos and stovepipes.

- Communicate clearly and often.

Key Considerations

- Ensure a continuous communication process with affected stakeholders—up, down, and across their various organizations.

Summary

<u>The Most Important Thing</u>: Integrating programs as a prerequisite for taking the presumptive approach, because of the diverse groups of people involved, programs that are already in place, the quantity and nature of the firearm crime related data to be collected, and the various methods used to process the data.

<u>The Next Step</u>: Institutionalization of the presumptive approach requires training and enforced directives. The next chapter discusses the fundamentals of task number three of *The 13 Critical Tasks*—Establishing a Formal Understanding and Reinforcing Directives.

7

Chapter

Task Three: Establishing a Formal Understanding and Reinforcing Directives

Why Establish a Formal Understanding and Reinforce Directives?

Violent crime is a people issue, as are the causes and solutions. That is, violent crimes are committed by people and the programs intended to address these crimes must be designed and implemented by people. These programs can be very complicated and require communication, understanding, collaboration, and strict adherence to certain procedures. Because of the nature and quantity of the data and the many people involved in the crime solving process, the institutionalization of the presumptive approach requires **a formalized understanding and reinforcement of the directives**.

This formalized understanding of the roles and responsibilities of the participants and what the program entails is required in order to effectively communicate it through various means and media. A formalized understanding will also help ensure program continuity, as responsible parties routinely come and go and their roles change for various reasons.

The documentation of a program and a directive signed by senior agency executives provide a number of substantial and sustainable benefits. Together they:

- Communicate the commitment of the agency to personnel at all levels and empower them to act.

- Provide for program continuity, regardless of personnel changes.

- Communicate the vision, mission, strategies, and tactics in a consistent manner.

- Define the roles and expectations for each participant.

- Establish protocols and procedures.

- Provide for performance measurement and the ability to adjust tactics and adapt to change.

A Memorandum of Understanding (MOU) signed by stakeholder agency executives can provide similar benefits between organizations.

Reinforcement of the program directives is also required in order to ensure the efficiency and effectiveness of ongoing operations in achieving their intended objectives. This reinforcement should be positive and supportive on the front end and should hold managers accountable for everyone doing their part on the back end.

Recommended Best Practices

Creating a Firearms Evidence Databank

The following pages outline a law the state of Connecticut created in order to create a firearm evidence data bank.

> CONNECTIUT GENERAL STATUTES
> TITLE 29 PUBLIC SAFETY AND STATE POLICE
> CHAPTER 529 DIVISION OF STATE POLICE
>
> **Sec. 29-7h. Firearms evidence databank.** (a) As used in this section:
>
> (1) "Firearms evidence databank" means a computer-based system that scans a test fire and stores an image of such test fire in a manner suitable for retrieval and comparison to other test fires and to other evidence in a case;
>
> (2) "Handgun" means any firearm capable of firing rim-fire or center-fire ammunition and designed or built to be fired with one hand;
>
> (3) "Laboratory" means the Division of Scientific Services forensic science laboratory within the Department of Public Safety;

(4) "Police department" means the Division of State Police within the Department of Public Safety or an organized local police department;

(5) "Test fire" means discharged ammunition consisting of a cartridge case or a bullet or a fragment thereof, collected after a handgun is fired and containing sufficient microscopical characteristics to compare to other discharged ammunition or to determine the handgun from which the ammunition was fired.

(b) (1) The Division of Scientific Services shall establish a firearms evidence databank. Test fire evidence submitted to the laboratory or collected from handguns submitted to the laboratory shall be entered into such databank in accordance with specific procedures adopted by the Commissioner of Public Safety, in the regulations adopted pursuant to subsection (f) of this section.

(2) The firearms evidence databank may be used by laboratory personnel to (A) compare two or more cartridge cases, bullets or other projectiles submitted to the laboratory or produced at the laboratory from a handgun, or (B) upon the request of a police department as part of a criminal case investigation, verify by microscopic examination any resulting match, and shall produce a report stating the results of such a search.

(3) Any image of a cartridge case, bullet or fragment thereof that is not matched by a search of the databank shall be stored in the databank for future searches.

(4) The Division of Scientific Services may permit a firearms section of a police department that complies with all laboratory guidelines and regulations adopted by the commissioner pursuant to subsection (f) of this section regarding the operation of the firearms evidence databank to (A) collect test fires from handguns that come into the custody of the police department, (B) set up a remote terminal to enter test fire images directly into the databank, and (C) search the databank.

(c) (1) Except as provided in subdivision (4) of subsection (b) of this section and subsection (d) of this section, a police department shall submit to the laboratory any handgun that comes into police custody as the result of a criminal investigation, as found property, or for destruction, prior to the return or the destruction of the handgun.

(2) The laboratory shall collect a test fire from each submitted handgun within sixty days of submission. The laboratory shall label the test fire with the handgun manufacturer, type of weapon, serial number, date of the test fire and name of the person collecting the test fire.

(d) (1) A police department shall collect a test fire from every handgun issued by that department to an employee not later than six months after October 1, 2001. On and after October 1, 2001, a police department shall collect a test fire from every handgun to be issued by that department before the handgun is so issued. Any police department may request the assistance of the Division of State Police or the laboratory to collect a test fire.

(2) The police department shall seal the test fire in a tamper-evident manner and label the package with the handgun manufacturer, handgun type, serial number and the name of the person collecting the test fire. The police department shall submit the test fire and two intact cartridges of the same type of ammunition used for the test fire to the laboratory.

(e) The laboratory may share the information in the firearms evidence   databank with other law enforcement agencies, both within and outside the state, and may participate in a national firearms evidence databank program.

(f) The commissioner shall adopt regulations, in accordance with the   provisions of chapter 54, to carry out the purposes of this section.

New Jersey's Attorney General Directive

The New Jersey Attorney General took the approach of leveraging the authority of the Office of the Attorney General to mandate that all law enforcement agencies follow a basic crime gun and evidence processing protocol.

State of New Jersey
OFFICE OF THE ATTORNEY GENERAL
DEPARTMENT OF LAW AND PUBLIC SAFETY
PO BOX 080
TRENTON NJ 08625-0080

JON S. CORZINE
Governor

ANNE MILGRAM
Attorney General

ATTORNEY GENERAL LAW ENFORCEMENT DIRECTIVE No. 2008-1

SUBMISSION AND ANALYSIS OF INFORMATION RELATING TO SEIZED AND RECOVERED FIREARMS

WHEREAS, Governor Jon S. Corzine has issued a strategy for Safe Streets and Neighborhoods that calls upon New Jersey's entire law enforcement community to respond to emerging threats of gun and gang violence, using state-of-the-art technologies, interjurisdictional information sharing and analysis systems, and the principles of intelligence-led policing to solve and deter gun-related crimes; and

WHEREAS, the State of New Jersey and the Federal Bureau of Alcohol, Tobacco Firearms, and Explosives (ATF) have entered into a partnership that provides the New Jersey State Police with real-time electronic access to data to trace the source of firearms recovered by law enforcement agencies across the State, allowing the State Police to use the ATF e-Trace System to identify trends, relationships between seemingly distinct crimes and transactions, source states, source vendors, and individuals who are importing or trafficking guns in New Jersey; and

WHEREAS, the successful implementation of any computerized information sharing and analysis system depends on the timely, accurate, and complete entry of all pertinent information into the database; and

WHEREAS, it is appropriate and cost-effective to take full advantage of the existing Criminal Justice Information System (CJIS), which is already used by all law enforcement agencies in the State, to transmit and receive information, and to establish a NJ Trace System that can link multiple law enforcement databases, including the National Crime Information Center (NCIC) System (which can ascertain whether a recovered firearm was reported stolen), the National Integrated Ballistics Identification Network (NIBIN) (which can reveal whether a recovered firearm is related to any other criminal episode or person), and the ATF e-Trace System (which discloses the identity of the recovered firearm's first purchaser, when it was purchased, and the retailer from whom it was purchased).

HUGHES JUSTICE COMPLEX ● TELEPHONE: (609) 292-4925 ● FAX: (609) 292-3508
New Jersey Is An Equal Opportunity Employer ● Printed on Recycled Paper and Recyclable

ATF NIBIN Memorandum

ATF administers the NIBIN program through funds appropriated for the purpose by Congress. ATF provides the NIBIN partners with technology, training, and communication lines. ATF is also responsible for the national coordination of the program. A Memorandum of Understanding between ATF and the NIBIN partner details the conditions under which this takes place and clearly outline the responsibilities, procedures, and expectations.

Appendix III

Example Memorandum of Understanding Between ATF and the NIBIN
Partner Agencies

MEMORANDUM OF UNDERSTANDING
Between the Bureau of Alcohol, Tobacco, Firearms and Explosives and
the Agency Name Regarding the
National Integrated Ballistic Information Network

This Memorandum of Understanding (MOU) is entered into by the U.S.
Department of Justice (DOJ), Bureau of Alcohol, Tobacco, Firearms and
Explosives (ATF), and the (Agency Name), hereinafter collectively
referred to as "the parties." The MOU establishes and defines a
partnership between the parties that will result in the installation,
operation, and administration of ATF integrated ballistics imaging systems
for the collection, analysis, and dissemination of crime gun data through
ATF's National Integrated Ballistic Information Network (NIBIN)
Program at the Agency.

AUTHORITY

This MOU is established pursuant to the authority of the participants to
engage in activities related to the investigation and suppression of violent
crimes involving firearms. ATF's authority is derived from, among other
things, the Gun Control Act of 1968 (as amended), 18 U.S.C. Chapter 44.

BACKGROUND

Violent crimes are being committed with firearms in the United States . A
firearm leaves unique, identifiable characteristics on expelled ammunition.
Firearms, expended bullets, and cartridge casings associated with crimes
are currently being collected and maintained as evidence by law
enforcement agencies. The ATF NIBIN Program assists Federal, state,
and local law enforcement agencies in combating firearms-related violence
through the use of Integrated Ballistics Identification System (IBIS)
technology to compare images of ballistic evidence (projectiles and

cartridge casings) obtained from crime scenes and recovered firearms.

SCOPE

Participation in this program is expressly restricted to the ballistic imaging of firearms data associated with crimes. NIBIN equipment provided and deployed by ATF to other Federal, State, or local law authorities may be used only for imaging of ballistic evidence and test fires of firearms taken into law enforcement custody.

NIBIN equipment deployed by ATF to Federal, state, or local authorities shall not be used to capture or store ballistic images acquired at the point of manufacture, importation, sale, law enforcement issued firearms not associated with crimes. Nothing in this MOU shall preclude State or local parties from capturing or storing such information in local ballistic imaging systems, provided that such local imaging systems shall not be connected to NIBIN without ATF's specific written approval, which must be consistent with current ATF authorization and appropriations restrictions and policy.

APPLICABLE LAWS

The applicable statutes, regulations, directives and procedures of the United States, DOJ, and ATF shall govern this MOU and all documents and actions pursuant to it.

Nothing in this MOU will prevail over any Federal law, regulation, or other Federal rule recognized by ATF.

This MOU does not grant any funding whatsoever. All specific actions agreed to herein shall be subject to funding and administrative or legislative approvals.

MODIFICATIONS AND TERMINATIONS

This MOU shall not affect any pre-existing or independent relationships or obligations between the parties. If any provision of this MOU is determined to be invalid or unenforceable, the remaining provisions shall remain in force and unaffected to the fullest extent permitted by law and regulation.

Except as provided herein, this MOU may be modified or amended only by written, mutual agreement of the parties. Either party may terminate this MOU by providing written notice to the other party. The termination shall be effective upon the thirtieth calendar day following notice, unless a later date is agreed upon.

If either party terminates this MOU, ATF will retain its interest in the NIBIN equipment and in the electronically stored information contained in the database. ATF agrees to provide to (Agency Name) an electronic copy of the data collected by (Agency Name).

INCORPORATION OF APPENDIX

The Appendix to this MOU includes definitions of terms used; requirements concerning NIBIN equipment; usage, movement, and removal of the equipment; Rapid Brass Identification (RBI) users and host Data Acquisition System (DAS) sites; maintenance of the equipment; security requirements; audits; personnel and training; and coordination of NIBIN efforts. Because these requirements may change over time due to technological advances, ;security enhancements, budgetary matters, and so forth, the Appendix may be occasionally updated. Parties to the MOU agree and understand that the Appendix is incorporated by reference as if fully stated herein. Execution of the MOU constitutes agreement to abide by the requirements and protocols set forth in the Appendix.

SIGNATORIES

The terms and conditions of this MOU will be considered accepted in their entirety upon the signature by ATF Division Director (SAC Name) and (LE Exec: Name), (LE Exec Title), representing (Agency Name).

LIABILITY

The (Agency Name) hereby agrees to assume full and sole liability for any damage, injury, or harm of any sort caused by the operation and use of any NIBIN equipment or related to the use and interpretation of any information contained in, processed by, or extracted from any data base subject to this agreement and the protocols and procedures of the, NIBIN Program.

No third party is intended to benefit or otherwise claim any rights whatsoever under this MOU. The rights and obligations set out in the

MOU run between the signatories to this MOU only.

AGREEMENT

ATF and the (Agency Name) hereby agree to abide by the terms and conditions of this MOU, including any appendices, and all policies of the NIBIN Program.

In witness thereof, the parties have hereby executed this MOU this _____ day of _____, _____.

_____

____

(SAC Name)   (LE Exec Name)
Division Director   (LE Exec Title)
Bureau of Alcohol, Tobacco,   (Agency Name)
Firearms and Explosives   (City/County/State)
(Field Division) Field Division

_____

___

Director, NIBIN Program
Bureau of Alcohol, Tobacco, Firearms and Explosives
Washington, DC

Appendix

TERMS

ATF - Bureau of Alcohol, Tobacco, Firearms and Explosives, a bureau within DOJ.

Bullets - Designated calibers of projectiles fired from rifles, revolvers and pistols.

Cartridge Casings - Designated metal casings from cartridges fired from rifles and revolvers and ejected from pistols.

Correlation - Automated data comparison of signature images to a database.

Crime Gun - A firearm that has been taken into police custody pursuant to a bonafide law enforcement investigation.

IBIS System - Any and all portions of an integrated/automated ballistic image processing system specifically defined as Integrated Ballistics Identification System (IBIS). This includes all the hardware and software that performs the complete function and/or generates data reports of results on the comparison of images of ballistic evidence (bullets and cartridge casings) obtained from crime scenes and recovered firearms.

NIBIN Equipment - Refers to integrated ballistics imaging, analysis, and information processing equipment wholly owned and provided by ATF.

NIBIN Network - An ATF designed and maintained system of interconnected computer systems and terminals used in support of the NIBIN Program and the IBIS System.

NIBIN Program - The management and administration of NIBIN, including the installation and utilization of the NIBIN equipment.

Security Requirements - Types and levels of protection necessary for equipment, data, information, applications, and facilities to meet security policies.

Security Policies - The set of laws, rules, directives and practices that regulate how an organization manage, protects and distributes controlled information.

Volunteers - Individuals who have chosen to perform gratuitous services and have entered into an agreement with the local NIBIN partner agency addressing all issues of confidentiality, costs and a waiver of all claims against the Federal government.

The (Agency Name) hereby agrees and acknowledges that an NIBIN equipment installed Flu maintained by ATF shall remain the property of

ATF and the U.S. Government.

ATF agrees to provide, install and maintain NIBIN equipment to the (Agency Name) for use by the (Agency Name) and any other law enforcement agencies served by or in partnership a with the; (Agency Name). The (Agency Name) may provide access to the NIBIN equipment under its operational control to any other law enforcement agency only pursuant to a written agreement in which such other law enforcement agency agrees to the same restrictions placed upon the (Agency Name) by this MOU. However, the (Agency Name) agrees to assume full liability and responsibility for the administration of such access.

Should the installation of the NIBIN equipment require physical construction at the site, (Agency Name) will be responsible for such construction and any costs associated therein.

MOVEMENT OF NIBIN EQUIPMENT

Any movement of the NIBIN equipment after the initial installation must be accomplished with prior written approval of ATF and at the expense of the (Agency Name).

In the event of unauthorized movement, alteration, damage, or destruction of any NIBIN equipment caused by its employees, contractors, or any other person under its control, the (Agency Name) agrees to assume the cost of replacement or repairs of the equipment.

The (Agency Name) agrees to report to ATF, within 5 working days, any incident involving an unauthorized movement, alteration, damage, or destruction of ATF-owned NIBIN equipment; any unauthorized use of NIBIN equipment; or the unauthorized release of data related to the NIBIN Program.

RAPID BRASS IDENTIFICATION (RBI) USERS AND HOST DATA ACQUISITION SYSTEM (DAS) SITES

ATF will provide and support primary communication lines necessary for connecting NIBIN equipment to the NIBIN network. The (Agency Name) agrees to assume complete liability and responsibility for the installation, use, and maintenance of any ancillary communication lines supporting an RBI system under its control.

MAINTENANCE OF NIBIN EQUIPMENT

ATF will maintain all NIBIN equipment furnished to the (Agency Name) and repair or replace inoperable or outdated equipment in an expeditious manner, subject to availability and funding. However, maintenance and repairs required as the result of unauthorized movement, alteration, damage, or destruction will not be assumed by ATF. The (Agency Name) agrees not to make or cause to be made any repairs, alterations, movements, additions, improvements, replacements, etc. to the NIBIN equipment not expressly authorized by ATF in advance, and further agrees to exercise due care in every respect to prevent movement, damage, destruction, or misuse of the equipment.

ATF further agrees to provide appropriate upgrades to the NIBIN equipment or related software in an expeditious manner, subject to availability and funding.

SECURITY REQUIREMENTS

The (Agency Name) will comply with all ATF, DOJ or other Federal security requirements related to the NIBIN equipment, NIBIN program, personnel, or NIBIN network. These requirements are set forth under NIBIN security policies. ATF will promptly notify the (Agency Name) should these requirements change.

The (Agency Name) agrees to conduct criminal background checks, including fingerprint checks, on all users of NIBIN DAS and RBI equipment. Upon successful completion of these background checks, (Agency Name) will notify the NIBIN Office in writing, verifying that the user is cleared, at least 30 days before the user is given access to the equipment.

REMOVAL OF NIBIN EQUIPMENT

ATF retains the right to remove the NIBIN equipment upon (1) its determination that the equipment is being neglected or misused; (2) or is not being used to a reasonable degree; (3) receipt of written notification of the termination of the participation of the (Agency Name) in the NIBIN Program; (4) termination of the NIBIN Program by ATF; (5) the cancellation of this MOU by ATF; or (6) failure to comply with any obligations or requirements set forth in this MOU. If ATF intends to remove the NIBIN equipment from the (Agency Name), ATF will provide written notice not less than 10 business days prior to the removal of the equipment.

AUDITS

ATF and the (Agency Name) acknowledge their understanding, that the operations described in this MOU are subject to audit by ATF; the Department of Justice, Office of the Inspector General; the General Accounting Office; and other auditors designated by the U.S. Government.

Such audits may include reviews of any and all records, documents, reports, accounts, invoices, receipts, or other evidence of expenditures related to this MOU and the NIBIN Program.

Further, all parties hereby agree to allow auditors to conduct one or more in-person interviews of any and all personnel the auditors have determined may have knowledge relevant to transactions performed or other matters involving this MOU and the NIBIN Program.

The (Agency Name) hereby acknowledges its understanding that, for accounting purposes, the principles and standards for determining costs shall be governed by the policies set forth in the Office of Management and Budget (OMB) Circular A-87, revised (available via the OMB, the Superintendent of Documents at the U.S. Government Printing Office, or via the Internet at

http://www.whitehouse.gov/omb/circulars/a087/aO87-all.html.)

PERSONNEL AND TRAINING

Prior to the execution of this MOU and Data Acquisition System/Remote (DAS/R) installation, the (Agency Name) must have a technical person on staff capable of performing forensic microscopic comparison of bullet and cartridge evidence. The Agency agrees to provide sufficient personnel to operate NIBIN equipment. This MOU should not be construed to require the hiring of any new personnel, except at the discretion of the (Agency Name). If the (Agency Name) determines that additional personnel resources are required, all costs associated with this hiring will be borne by Agency. Volunteers must satisfy the ;same requirements as other users of the NIBIN equipment, and be properly trained, qualified and approved in advance by ATF.

The (Agency Name) will ensure that only trained, cleared and qualified personnel operate the ATF-owned NIBIN equipment and that only trained and qualified instructors use the NIBIN equipment for the training of new personnel. Training must be conducted by ATF or ATF authorized personnel.

Use of the NIBIN equipment will be under the management and control of the (Agency Name).

Contingent on sufficient funding, ATF agrees to provide training for users of the NIBIN equipment at the discretion of ATF.

USAGE OF NIBIN EQUIPMENT

The (Agency Name) shall enter bullets and cartridge cases related to crimes recovered by law enforcement into the NIBIN system. Because the NIBIN Program focuses on the reduction of firearms-related violent crimes such as homicides and assaults, ATF particularly encourages the (Agency Name) to enter ballistic images of evidence recovered from violent crime scenes into the NIBIN system.

ATF also encourages inclusion of all test-fired evidence from seized firearms. In addition, because certain calibers (including .25 auto, .32 auto, .380 auto, 9mm, .38/.357, 10mm/.40 S&W, and .45 auto) make up the vast majority of crime guns, the (Agency Name) will image as much recovered and test-fired evidence from such firearms as is practical. Nothing in the MOU precludes the (Agency Name) from entering test-fired evidence from firearms of additional calibers.

COORDINATION

ATF and the (Agency Name) agree to adhere to standardized procedures and policies for collecting, handling, documenting, transporting, and preserving firearms, bullets, casings, and any similar evidence submitted for analysis and input into the NIBIN equipment.

ATF and the (Agency Name) similarly agree to adhere to standardized procedures and policies for the source data collection, input, exchange, and protection of information, to include information as to the location where ballistics evidence was collected, the circumstances under which it was collected, and all crimes to which the firearm(s) or other ballistics evidence is linked.

ATF and (Agency Name) agree to cooperate in the development and implementation of data entry protocols and quality assurance procedures for the NIBIN Program. ATF further agrees to cooperate with all participants in the NIBIN Program to establish model standards, protocols, and procedures for the users of the network equipment and system. Such protocols will be applicable as they are implemented.

The (Agency Name) will require all participating law enforcement agencies to adhere to the protocols, procedures, policies, and quality assurance standards as established above.

The (Agency Name) agrees to provide ATF with monthly reports outlining historical, statistical, and case adjudication information on the use, and results of the use, of the NIBIN equipment and the related services provided by ATF and the manufacturer of the equipment. Additionally, the (Agency Name) agrees to provide ATF with an estimate of the overall percentage of recovered and test-fired evidence available that was entered into the NIBIN system at the end of each calendar year. Such information will be gathered for the purpose of informing the law enforcement community, other Government agencies, Congress; and the public on the successes of the NIBIN Program. Additionally, ATF will use the information to attempt to collect data for results-oriented performance measures.

Cincinnati Police New Procedure

Below is a revision to Cincinnati Police Procedure 12.720.

For more information you can refer to:
www.cincinnati-oh.gov/police/downloads/police_pdf35554.pdf

Cincinnati Police Department

Colonel Thomas H. Streicher, Jr., Police Chief

January 20, 2009

12.720 <u>EVIDENCE: SUBMITTING FOR PHYSICAL ANALYSIS</u>

Reference:

Procedure 12.130 - Vice Control and Enforcement Responsibilities

Procedure 12.715 – Property and Evidence: Confiscation, Accountability, Processing, Storage, and Release

Procedure 12.725 Blood drying Rooms: Processing of evidence Exposed to Blood Borne Pathogens

Manual of Rules and Regulations - 2.04

Forensics Manual

Investigative Manual, 2.4.0 and 13.1.15

Purpose:

Prevent the suppression of evidence and dismissal of cases on procedural grounds.

Policy:

Evidence submitted for physical analysis will be processed in a consistent manner in order to maintain a high standard of dependability for examination of the sample. The officer will record all pertinent information on the Hamilton County Coroner's Laboratory Evidence Submission Form.

Procedure:

- Alcoholic Evidence ...

- Drug Evidence ...

- DNA Evidence ...

- Other Evidence Requiring Physical Analysis.

Criminalistics will:

- Respond to the Court Property room to check out any firearm submitted that has not been processed and they will:

- Attempt to lift all latent fingerprints from the firearm.

- Process quality prints through the Automated Fingerprint Identification System (AFIS) and report their results to the Special Investigations Squad (SIS) personnel.

- Test fire the firearm and report their results to SIS.

- Take the firearm to the Hamilton County Coroner's Crime Lab for National Integrated Ballistic Identification Network (NIBIN) test firing.

- The Crime Lab will report to the Criminalistics Squad both positive and negative results of the NIBIN searches.

Critical Elements

- Documentation the program and directives thoroughly—from high level vision and strategy to ground level tactical execution and day-to-day operations.

- Ensure that the policy directive is issued from the appropriate level of authority (e.g., agency, administrative, legislative).

- Create formal MOUs to allow for the participation in joint operations between various independent stakeholder organizations.

- Establish an internal review mechanism with senior mangers held accountable for their subordinate's adherence to the directives.

- Communication clearly and frequently.

Key Considerations

- Ensure that the policies and procedures are achievable and sustainable and balanced in terms of people, processes, and technology.

- Communicate continuously with affected stakeholders up, down, and across their various organizations.

- Consider ways to maximize the reach and range of the directives by leveraging the power of the state (e.g., Office of the Attorney General) and the legislature (e.g., laws).

Summary

The Most Important Thing: Creating standard operating directives to advance the concept of the presumptive approach in which the responsible parties are held accountable for following.

The Next Step: The next chapter discusses the fundamentals of task number four of *The 13 Critical Tasks*—Collecting Firearm and Related Evidence.

8
Chapter

Task Four: Collecting Firearm and Related Evidence

Why Collect Firearm and Related Evidence?

The early chapters of this book covered the fact that valuable data for taking the presumptive approach is found inside **and** outside a gun.

The inside of the gun provides ballistic data in the form of unique markings left on fired ammunition components by the internal working parts of a gun. In addition, other valuable forensic data, such as DNA, fingerprints, and hairs and fibers which can help police identify the gun possessor can be found on the surface bearing areas of the firearm and ammunition components.

The outside of the gun provides identifying data in the form of make, model, and serial number that can be used to track the transactional history of the gun. This data is regulatory rather than criminal in nature. It is generated and maintained in accordance with the laws and regulations that have been established to manage legitimate commerce in arms. For example, every gun made in the United States must, by law, bear certain identifying information which is visible on the **outside,** such as the name and location of the manufacturer and a unique serial number. In addition, gun manufacturers and dealers must keep certain records to document their firearm acquisition and disposition transactions during the regular course of their business. It is this type of transactional data that is generated and maintained over time which, if readily accessible, allows for the performance of what is commonly referred as a crime gun trace. Simply put, police can trace the history of a recovered crime gun by following the paper trail of firearm transactions from the day the gun was manufactured to its first retail sale. Sometimes the information gained from a single crime gun trace can have immediate tactical investigative value when trying to identify who fired the "smoking gun".

Valuable trace evidence can also be found on fired ammunition components and firearms. For example, a bullet's surface may contain minute paint chips indicating that it may have struck an object with a painted surface before striking the victim. Any protocols put in place should also account for trace evidence collection.

Crime gun trace data collected over time can help police and policy makers identify patterns and trends that are of value when developing new strategies and policies to keep guns out of the hands of criminals.

The generation and maintenance of this type of non-crime related data which is integral to crime gun tracing most often requires legislative authorization and ongoing regulatory control.

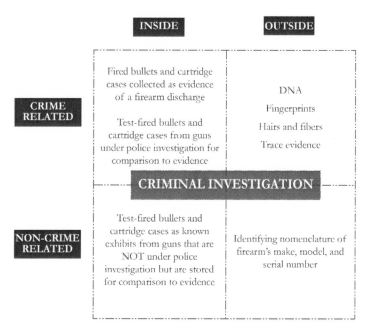

As illustrated in the figure above, all crime related and non-crime related data that is found inside and outside the gun is paramount to the presumptive approach. It must be collected, processed, and well managed to generate both strategic and timely tactical crime-solving actions aimed at reducing urban gun and gang violence.

The ability to sustain these actions becomes the challenge and the solution lies in a balance of people, processes, and technology. Think of creating this balance in terms of the three-legged stool discussed in chapter 3. For example, if the desired process of test-firing every gun taken into police custody is truly unsustainable because the people or technology legs of the stool are too short, then balance the stool by shortening the process leg and do not test fire every gun. The trick then is to decide which guns get test fired and which do not. In other words, the task is to identify the types of firearms that are most often being used in crime. Historical gun trace data is useful for this purpose, providing that the data set is comprehensive and not skewed. Properly conducted crime gun tracing studies have been very accurate in identifying the types of guns that are most likely to be used in crimes within particular regions and by certain age groups.

Sometimes the people and process legs of the stool can be balanced through the integration of technology. For example, today, automated ballistic identification technology like IBIS can easily perform a process—that was previously thought to be unsustainable—which quickly and effectively searches a piece of ballistic evidence against thousands of other pieces of evidence in order to help law enforcement find more potential crime solving leads.

There is an obligation placed upon police administrators today to spend money in ways that produce best value outcomes. Because of advances in technology, forensic ballistic evidence can now be viewed in terms of a sustainable process with a high probability for the successful generation of investigative leads. IBIS technology can correlate evidence at speeds well beyond human capacity and exchange data quickly across multisystem networks like NIBIN. NIBIN has been proven to be very effective at generating actionable information to help the partnering police agencies solve more gun related crimes within single, and across multiple, police jurisdictions.

Therefore, it becomes a critical task to collect and enter **every feasible** piece of ballistic evidence into the system in order to benefit investigations, intelligence, and the value of the technology investment as well.

What happens when some jointly affected stakeholders institute processes to collect this comprehensive data while others do not? Read on.

A Case Study: McCalla, Alabama

In March 1996, the Jefferson County Sheriff's Office investigated a home invasion that became a robbery resulting in the murder of Hazel Love, a 68-year-old woman in McCalla, Alabama. Investigators recovered several discharged cartridge cases at the scene and, later, bullets at the autopsy. The evidence was submitted to the Alabama Department of Forensic Sciences (ADFS) lab in Birmingham. IBIS operators at the ADFS lab entered the evidence into the NIBIN database.

In September 2000, police in Adamsville, Alabama, conducted an investigation of a felon who was in unlawful possession of a firearm. At the time, a firearm was retained as evidence and placed on a shelf in the police department's property room.

In December 2002, Birmingham Police investigating a home invasion learned of the firearm stored in Adamsville. Investigators requested a NIBIN check on the firearm. Two weeks later, the ADFS Lab surprisingly reported that there was no NIBIN link to the Birmingham home invasion but there was indeed a link between the Adamsville firearm and the 1996 murder of Hazel Love in McCalla. The match was later confirmed by a firearm expert.

In February 2003, the Jefferson County Sheriff's Office arrested two men that were linked to the Adamsville firearm for the murder of Hazel Love as well as for serious crimes across the county. One of the suspects is now serving multiple life sentences without the chance of parole.

This case demonstrates the need for the collection and sharing of ballistic data from crime scenes and firearms seized by police within the affected crime region—until this was done the murder of Hazel Love murder remained unsolved. One department's forgotten evidence is another department's crucial evidence. In this case, neither department knew of the other's evidence.

Recommended Best Practices

Boston Police Policy for Ballistics Evidence Collection

The Boston Police Department, Rules and Procedures state that:

> Ballistics evidence shall be delivered as soon as possible to the Ballistics Unit. Whenever possible, photographs, crime scene measurements and sketches should be made. Whenever there is doubt as to the proper handling of firearms and related evidence, the Ballistics Unit should be contacted. Bullets found embedded in surfaces and materials shall only be removed by Ballistics Unit personnel. The Boston Police Department, Rules and Procedures state that:

> Firearms coming into the possession of police officers shall be properly documented on a designated Firearm Submission Form. An incident report will also be completed documenting all facts including whether the person found in possession held a valid permit for the weapon. Firearms shall be handled in a safe manner keeping in mind that firearms and related evidence are also processed for latent fingerprints. Firearms and related evidence is delivered to the police district offices in which the incident occurred and secured there until delivered by a designated supervisor to the central Ballistics Unit. Under no circumstances shall a firearm or other ballistics evidence be released to an outside agency until the Ballistics Unit has had an opportunity to examine it. Copies of all incidents reports involving firearms will be forwarded to the Commander of the firearms licensing unit for appropriate action or forwarding to the affected licensing authority if located outside of Boston.

New York Police—A Central Repository

The New York City Police Department has a policy in which all firearms and firearm related evidence is sent to a single centralized ballistics unit for examination, entry into IBIS, and gun tracing. The NYPD has established partnership agreements with other federal, state, and local law enforcement agencies operating within the jurisdiction of the city to submit all of their firearms and firearm related evidence to the NYPD Ballistics Unit.

West Palm Beach Police Department Firearms Protocol

The West Palm Beach Firearms Protocol focuses primarily on ballistics and gun tracing. The procedures contained in the protocol are broken down into three main categories:

1. **Procedures for the Collection of Crime Guns and Crime Gun Related Evidence**; These include the following: Guns Actually Used in a Crime & Recovered on the Crime Scene -No handling of guns by patrol officers without gloves -Crime Scene Investigator will photograph weapon -Crime Scene Investigator will collect & process fingerprint & DNA Guns Recovered Due to a Traffic Stop or Suspect Stop/Search Found Property Guns

2. **Procedures for Processing All Recovered Crime Guns and Crime Gun Evidence**; These include the following: The crime gun(s) will be traced. The crime gun(s) and ammunition will be submitted for test-firing and entry into NIBIN. All bullet projectiles and/or ammunition casings recovered at all crime/shooting scenes shall be submitted. The crime gun(s) and ammunition will be processed with swabs for the presence of DNA and treated with superglue fumes to assist in preserving any existing latent fingerprints for identification.

3. **Procedures for Processing All Crime Gun Arrests**; These include the following: The arresting officer should try to personally fingerprint the defendant prior to leaving them at the jail. The arresting officer should try to personally obtain a DNA swab sample from the arrestee. Document all statements by the defendant regarding his/her possession of the firearm. Prepare a detailed narrative report regarding the arrest. Obtain a criminal history printout for the defendant. NIBIN, Crime Gun Tracing, DNA, Prints, Stolen cars

Taking a Stand: Reducing Gun Violence in Our Communities

This comprehensive report was produced by the International Association of Chiefs of Police (IACP) 2007 Great Lakes Summit on Gun Violence. It recommends a number of best practices for taking the presumptive approach. Recommendations 27 and 30 directly relate to the collection of ballistic and crime gun trace data. Below are some selected excerpts from each:

Recommendation 27:
Congress should fund the National Integrated Ballistic Information Network (NIBIN) and law enforcement agencies should use it consistently; it should also be funded to become integrated nation-wide.

> *...Through NIBIN and in coordination with ATF, state, local and tribal law enforcement agencies can enter the fired bullets and cartridge cases recovered from crime scenes into the Integrated Ballistics Information [Identification] System (IBIS) database to determine whether the ballistic evidence from that particular crime gun matches the evidence from any other crime scene. Matching ballistic evidence across crimes allows law enforcement to identify patterns of crime gun use, solve gun crimes (including crimes that have remained unsolved over several years) and disrupt illegal gun trafficking. NIBIN enables law enforcement to combat crimes—including gang crimes— where frequent incidents of gun violence may be conclusively linked and establish a case for prosecution. Ideally, NIBIN allows law enforcement to follow guns wherever the guns themselves are used and to connect crimes that might have never been connected, whether because of geography, jurisdictions with their own separate intelligence databases or other factors. It is recommended that all law enforcement agencies partner with ATF to ensure that a robust forensic database is built and continuously maintained.*

Recommendation 30:
Every law enforcement agency should use E-Trace, ensure that officers know how to properly recover and process crime guns and make sure that officers trace all firearms recovered:

> *. . . Then they must generate a comprehensive description of the gun. This description should include serial number, manufacturer, type of firearm, caliber, model and any distinguishing features. This description, entered into the National Crime Information Center (NCIC), may yield critical information including whether the gun has been reported lost or stolen or was used in a previous crime. Such information is invaluable to officers interacting with individuals at the scene of a crime, or investigating the crime long afterwards. Ensuring that officers are knowledgeable about NCIC and the way in which records must be submitted and received will ensure agency success in handling crime guns as tools for solving crimes. The requirement, established by the Gun Control Act of 1968, that all guns manufactured or imported into the U.S. contain a serial number and the name, city and state of the gun's manufacturer assists law enforcement in tracing the gun's history. The accurate identification and tracing of recovered firearms is one of the most important steps in a criminal gun investigation. Tracing every recovered crime gun will eventually reveal previously unidentified persons or suspects, addresses*

and other critical associations. Comprehensive tracing facilitates the development of a database that tracks each traced gun from manufacturer to the wholesaler and eventually to the FFL, who by law must identify the first known purchaser of that gun. In conjunction with ATF's Firearms Tracing System (FTS), which contains millions of records such as prior traces, lost or stolen guns, multiple handgun sales, and interstate firearms shipments, a trace can yield information that is critical in solving many crimes, such as firearms trafficking, straw purchases or an FFL who has falsified a sale or has failed to provide accurate information on purchasers, homicides and gang shootings. Law enforcement executives should commit their agencies, through written policy, to tracing guns using the best means available, including E-Trace. Maintained by the National Tracing Center Division (NTC) of ATF, E-Trace allows law enforcement agencies to make trace requests and receive the results of those requests over the Internet. E-Trace, available only to accredited agencies, enables them to expedite traces, pursue multiple traces and review all trace results at once. It is imperative that agencies learn to trace all guns through NTC and also strive to become accredited to receive E-Trace.

Critical Elements

- Collaborate with affected stakeholders to identify a sustainable and timely process for following the use of the presumptive approach in the collection of information from inside and outside a crime gun by balancing people, processes and technology.

- At a bare minimum establish a protocol to: (1) test fire all guns taken into police custody of certain specified types and calibers that data indicates are most likely to be used in crime, (2) enter all test fired exhibits and all recovered ballistic evidence of corresponding calibers using an automated ballistic identification technology like IBIS and NIBIN, and (3) trace all[14] guns taken into police custody using an electronic information management system like ATF eTrace or IBIS Firecycle.

---

[14] All guns, without exception, should be traced; picking and choosing certain guns risks skewing the data. This information may be needed to make policy and resource balancing decisions.

- Thoroughly document the protocol for data collection and integrate it into the standard operating procedures within agencies and through a formal MOU across agencies operating within the same affected crime area.

Key Considerations

- Identify the various police, forensic, and prosecutorial agencies that are joint stakeholders operating within the same affected crime area.

- Determine the crime gun trace capability of the jurisdictions. Are the laws and regulations in place that enable the collection of and access to non-crime related information related to the legitimate commerce of firearms and their acquisition and disposition.

- Evaluate the adequacy of the data collection processes in terms of identification, integrity, handling, storage, quality, and input and output processing times.

Summary

The Most Important Thing: Collecting the many types of data that should be part of any presumptive approach, such as ballistic data, crime gun trace Data, DNA, fingerprints, hairs, fibers, and even acoustic data used to pinpoint the location of firearm discharges.

The Next Step: The collection of data and evidence is one thing, but getting it to where it needs to be processed is another. The next chapter discusses the fundamentals of task number five of *The 13 Critical Tasks*— Transferring Evidence.

9
Chapter

Task Five: Transferring Evidence

Why Transfer Evidence?

On the surface this task is fairly straightforward. An item of property collected at a crime scene, or otherwise taken into police custody, must be transferred to skilled personnel at a lab or other facility (e.g., Ballistics Unit, Bureau of Identification, etc.) that is properly equipped to conduct the required examinations. However, depending upon a number of factors, such as proximity of services, staffing, funding, organizational culture, and standard operating procedures—or the lack thereof—the transfer of property can present many challenging obstacles when attempting to follow the presumptive approach. Acting in the spirit of collaboration and determination, the stakeholders can overcome these challenges together. The goal here is to embed a sustainable solution that meets the timeliness requirements of all of the stakeholders. This may call for the better balancing of people, processes, and technology, and changes in organizational behavior and procedures. The redistribution of certain generic tasks may be necessary in order to better balance workloads, maximize expert resources, and accelerate processes.

The IBIS FastTRAX Pilot Project: Redistribution of Test-firing and Data Entry Tasks

In January of 2007, Forensic Technology entered into a four-way partnership with ATF, the Virginia DFS—Eastern Laboratory, and the Norfolk Police Department to conduct a field test of their **IBIS®** FastTRAX™ services concept.

The Inputs

ATF approved the technical solution, granted network access, and performed the initial pilot project quality review. The Virginia DFS— Eastern Lab set quality protocols, provided hit confirmation review, and reported confirmed hits to the Norfolk PD. The Norfolk PD performed the test-firing of 372 seized auto-loading pistols, submitted the test fired exhibits to Forensic Technology's facility in Florida, and followed-up on the investigative leads provided by FastTRAX services in the form of IBIS/NIBIN hits. Forensic Technology acquired the test fired cartridge cases, entered the data into IBIS, searched the NIBIN database, reviewed the results, and forwarded recommendations back to the Norfolk Police and the Virginia DFS—Eastern Laboratory.

The Outputs

From among the 372 test fires involved in the pilot project, Forensic Technology reported seven associations or high confidence matches to the lab and the Norfolk PD within five to seven business days. Overall, based on the data produced during the processing of the 372 firearms by each of the process partners, FastTRAX required 50 percent fewer man-hours in comparison with the current standard method used to process test fires. **In roughly 10 weeks, the pilot project reduced the equivalent of seven months of data backlogs.**

The Outcomes

Within the first two weeks, one of the FastTRAX matches helped the Norfolk PD arrest a gang member for murder. Another FastTRAX match to a gun taken into custody by Norfolk PD was linked to a shooting under investigation in a nearby police jurisdiction. The link provided the other agency with valuable information about the shooting being investigated. Note that this situation represents a very common scenario in which police agency "A" takes a gun into custody and stores it in their property room, unaware that the gun is a sought-after weapon for a murder that police agency "B" is investigating. It underscores the need for regional protocols.

The Norfolk PD was able to find a sustainable way in which to restart its practice of routinely submitting test fires for forensic analysis. In fact, they had stopped sending guns to the lab for test-firing because of the long turnaround times. The Virginia DFS—Eastern Laboratory's forensic experts were able to concentrate on processing crime scene evidence rather than spending time creating cases for 372 submitted firearms in order to test fire them. The forensic experts at the lab saved time by not having to process test fires that would produce no information for investigators. Instead, the pilot project allowed the lab to focus its limited resources on the seven high confidence matches provided by FastTRAX. These matches had a very high potential to provide investigative leads to the detectives investigating the related crimes.

Estimating a processing time of 1.25 hours for the lab to complete the required test fire process of a firearm, the lab saved almost 500 hours of precious resource time by not having to process all 372 firearms. The NIBIN program gained more data, and thus provided more value to the NIBIN partners. The pilot project provided Forensic Technology with the opportunity to test the feasibility of the FastTRAX concept, design sustainable processes to execute it repeatedly, and fully understand the inputs and outputs required in order to make FastTRAX a sustainable service offering.

The Conclusions

- FastTRAX helped generate more timely and actionable investigative leads and helped stimulate collaboration between detectives and forensic experts.

- FastTRAX helped reduce the evidence processing backlogs of the involved police agency and crime lab.

- FastTRAX helped give broader access to advanced technology, like IBIS, to more law enforcement agencies.

- FastTRAX helped more police agencies participate as NIBIN partners and derive more benefits from it.

- FastTRAX showed that more crimes can be solved when the evidence of one agency is shared among other agencies.

- FastTRAX helped save all of the participants significant amounts of time by allowing them to focus on doing what they do best, rather than wasting time on the performance of non-optimized processes.

- FastTRAX proved to be an effective tool that can help criminal justice stakeholders balance the people, processes, and technology required to successfully deal with escalating levels of firearm related crime.

When dealing with ballistics, crime gun tracing, fingerprints, and DNA, ways must be found to overcome the time and distance factors involved in getting firearms and related evidence where they need to go. Collaborative thinking and action among the stakeholders will lead to a solution. The FastTRAX program is exemplary of collaborative thinking and actions.

Stakeholders occupying a position of authority in the criminal justice chain can encourage and influence stakeholders at each level of collaboration required. For example, in Washington D.C., there's a story going around that many years ago firearm evidence didn't always make it to the Ballistics Unit. This sometimes resulted in problems for the prosecutors who were caught off guard in front of juries with crime guns that were inoperable or did not meet the legal definitions. The problem disappeared when the prosecutor's office refused to open a criminal case on any firearm that was not accompanied by a statement from an expert witness who would testify as to the gun's ability to expel a projectile by action of an explosive.

The core message is simple: Every crime gun holds potentially crime solving information—it cannot be exploited from the property room shelf.

Recommended Best Practices

Designate Responsible Vault Custodians

Many agencies appoint evidence vault custodians who are responsible for controlling access to the vault, maintaining evidence accountability, ensuring that policies and procedures are followed, and protecting and maintaining the vault environment. Vault custodian assignments may be full-time in nature or assigned as ancillary duties. Periodic inventories should be conducted by two disinterested parties who are not vault custodians. When vault custodians change assignments and new ones are appointed, an inventory should be conducted and any discrepancies resolved before responsibility for the vault is passed to the new vault custodian.

Walk-in Wednesday Program—Los Angeles Police Department

The LAPD Firearms Analysis Unit has developed "Walk-in Wednesdays"—a unique approach to providing timely information to investigators. Negating the need to complete evidence transmittal reports and ship and transport evidence, the project allows investigators to walk their ballistic evidence into the lab at certain appointed times when firearm examiners are on duty. The examiners screen the evidence, enter it into IBIS, search the NIBIN database, and provide immediate feedback to the investigators. Within 24 hours, the lab provides investigators with feedback on the results of the IBIS correlations. The program quickly puts investigative information in the hands of detectives for immediate follow-up and corroboration. The program has worked extremely well for LAPD and other agencies have adopted it as well.

Note: As of this writing, the LAPD is working with property room custodians to develop a protocol that eliminates the initial step of having the detectives walk evidence into the lab.

Open Case File—Allegheny County Medical Examiner

The Allegheny County Medical Examiner's lab provides forensic services for a number of law enforcement agencies within the county. The agreement with submitters of ballistic evidence is that the evidence will be retained by the lab until such time that the case is disposed of or the submitting agency instructs otherwise. This practice is designed to eliminate the need for time- and resource-wasting callbacks of evidence. For example, the practice in many areas of the country is to summit fired bullets and evidence to the lab. The lab will examine and process the evidence through IBIS and a network like NIBIN and, if there is no further need to hold on to the evidence, it is returned to the submitting agency. Subsequently, new evidence is submitted by the same agency or another agency, or a gun is sent in for test-firing and processing through IBIS. When the new evidence or test fires are processed through IBIS, it frequently happens that the new evidence or test fires appear to have similarities to the evidence that was previously submitted and then returned. Now, the lab has to issue a callback for this prior evidence to be returned for comparison with the new evidence. This callback procedure takes time and resources on the part of the lab and the police agency. It has been reported during *The 13 Critical Tasks Workshops* that the callback process could take from days to weeks to months and that it is not unusual for the same evidence to be called back multiple times. Not only do callbacks waste time and resources, they expose the evidence to loss and damage and can leave its integrity in question. Maintaining an open case file of the evidence on behalf of the submitting agency until it is no longer needed avoids these pitfalls.

Critical Elements

- Map the property custody process and identify any time and distance obstacles that impede the timely exploitation of information from crime guns and related evidence.

- Balance people, processes, and technology to design a timely, efficient, and sustainable solution for managing and eliminating the gaps that hinder getting evidence from the point of custody to the applicable forensic and analysis units.

- Document the new process and implement it as standard policy.

Key Considerations

- When balancing people, processes, and technology, consider redistributing traditional workloads to prevent bottlenecks at the lab. For example, using crime scene technicians to lift fingerprints and DNA from guns and evidence and conducting test-firing outside the lab.

- Avoid the ping-ponging of evidence between the seizing agency and the lab for comparison callbacks—it wastes time.

- Consider extending the new process to all agencies within the affected crime region.

Summary

The Most Important Thing: Avoiding delays in the transfer of evidence and property to the lab, and embedding a sustainable solution that meets the timeliness requirements of all of the stakeholders, even if it means changes to organizational behavior and procedures.

The Next Step: The next chapter discusses the fundamentals of task number six of *The 13 Critical Tasks*—Assessing and Evaluating Evidence.

10
Chapter

Task Six: Assessing and Evaluating Evidence

Why Assess and Evaluate Evidence?

This task can reinforce the value of taking the presumptive approach by providing an opportunity for the forensic specialist and the investigator to collaborate and exchange timely and valuable information. For example, if a firearm examiner can tell from the pass examination of over a dozen fired cartridge cases that two different pistols of the same make and caliber were involved, he or she could inform the detectives at this juncture. Why wait weeks until the lab report is complete to communicate this fact to detectives?

Another example of improved communication at this step could be a scenario in which the detective knows that one of the suspects associated with the seized gun under examination at the lab has strong ties to another region. With this information, the lab would know to query the ballistic database in the other region to learn if the gun in question was used in a crime there.

This juncture could also serve as a decision gate where the facts and circumstances would be compared against a decision matrix to determine the protocols or the next steps to be followed. For example, some labs have a protocol in which, if a set of circumstances are met, the gun in question will be test fired, entered into IBIS, and queried against the NIBIN database <u>before</u> any additional firearm workups are done.

Also, depending on the best practice adopted, or on a proprietary process that is designed in-house, decisions can be made at this point to prepare for the upcoming test-firing and acquisition processes. For example, consider a firearm that has arrived at the lab for test-firing. With submitted items in hand, the examiner can begin to make decisions as to which type of ammunition to test fire with. If the firearm was loaded at the time of seizure and those cartridge cases were submitted along with the firearm, the examiner may choose to select the same type of ammunition for test-firing; the probability exists that the same type of ammunition would have been discharged from that gun during the commission of a crime. If no ammunition accompanied the gun, the examiner may then need to fall back on a protocol calling for a preselected standard type of ammunition to be used.

This juncture is also an opportunity for program integration with other forensic disciplines, crime gun tracing activities, and serial number restoration programs. It is also a good time to revisit the possibility of the presence of trace evidence (e.g., paint) on the submitted exhibits and how it will be collected and processed.

Overall this task provides an opportunity to fine-tune the presumptive approach as necessary, based on the facts at hand in order to optimize the remainder of the processes associated with this critical task.

Recommended Best Practices

Tentative Results Using Scientific Technology (TRUST)—Los Angeles Police Department

The LAPD Firearms Analysis Unit developed a unique approach to providing preliminary and timely information to investigators called Tentative Results Using Scientific Technology (TRUST). Investigators are provided with information based on IBIS correlation scores and visual on-screen examinations by firearm examiners as to probable but unconfirmed evidence links at that point in time. The information is carefully and clearly qualified as non-conclusive.

Typically, the way that TRUST works is that investigators are given a degree of probability that two gun crimes may be linked, and then they look for other information known to be true for both incidents to establish a connection. For example, investigators are told that there is a probability that crime A and crime B are linked by the same gun. In crime A, a man was shot by a robber and lived. In crime B, two suspects were arrested for illegal gun possession. Investigators use data other than the firearm data to establish a connection between the two crimes and solve crime A. They show photos of the arrested persons in crime B to the victim of the robbery and shooting in crime A. The victim identifies one of the men in the arrest photos as the person who shot him. An arrest warrant is obtained based on the statement and identification by the victim. The ballistic evidence never came into play.

The LAPD TRUST program, operating in conjunction with their Walk-in Wednesday program, has proven very effective in helping them to deal with the high levels of gun- and gang-related violent crime.

Rapid Assessment for IBIS Selection Examination (RAISE)— Ontario Center of Forensic Science (CFS)

The Ontario Center for Forensic Science (CFS) designed a protocol to strike a balance between the need to quickly generate investigative leads in shooting investigations and the need to conduct thorough forensic analysis in cases that are already bound for court. It involves a speedy "go straight to IBIS" procedure for certain situations where very little information is known. In other words, RAISE is used to ferret out valuable crime solving information from seemingly insignificant data. This is how it works:

To conduct preliminary examinations on fired ammunition components submitted under the Rapid Assessment for IBIS Selection Examination (RAISE) initiative for the purposes of:

- Selecting representative items for submission to the IBIS Unit at CFS for upload to the Canadian Integrated Ballistics Identification Network (CIBIN) database.

- Identifying linkages to other shooting occurrences/recovered firearms.

Items submitted for examination under the RAISE initiative must meet the following requirements:

- No accused/suspect has been identified.

- Only fired ammunition components (bullets and cartridge cases/shot shells) are to be examined.

- The occurrence is not a homicide.

- The requested examination is to determine whether the submitted items are linked to another shooting occurrence/recovered firearm (there is no request to know the caliber, type or number of firearms that discharged the fired ammunition components).

- No specific cross-reference is requested.

A full examination will not be conducted and a report will not be issued for items submitted under the RAISE initiative. A letter will be issued to advise the submitting agency that following a preliminary examination representative item(s) have been selected and transferred to the IBIS Unit for upload to the CIBIN database.

Suspicious Firearms Index (SFI)—Ontario Center of Forensic Science (CFS)

The SFI initiative has been implemented to enable police agencies to determine whether a seized/recovered firearm is linked to a shooting occurrence through the upload of test fired ammunition components to the CIBIN database. All SFI cases are conducted by the IBIS Unit of the CFS. Submissions under this initiative consist of either a seized/recovered commercial firearm or agency generated test fired ammunition components.

Items submitted for examination under the SFI initiative must meet the following requirements:

- One firearm per submission (or test fired ammunition components from one firearm).

- The firearm is in firing condition or may be easily restored to firing condition.

- The requested examination is to determine whether the firearm is linked to another shooting occurrence - no other examination is requested and classification of the firearm must be done by the police agency prior to submission.

- No specific cross-reference is requested.

- The firearm has been commercially manufactured - no improvised firearms (including homemade firearms and drilled-out starters pistols/revolvers), pellet or flare guns will be accepted.

NIBIN First—New York Police Department

To reduce and prevent ballistic case backlogs, the NYPD enacted a policy which in effect uses NIBIN to prioritize the unit's case work. When fired bullet and cartridge case evidence comes into the lab, the evidence is immediately entered into IBIS and searched through the NIBIN network. The evidence is then resealed and stored. The result of the IBIS search determines which evidence receives priority for further workup.

Color Coded Ammunition—Trinidad and Tobago

The government of Trinidad and Tobago color codes the ammunition destined for military, police and civilian use. Fired ammunition found at crime scenes is readily identifiable as originally intended for one of those three groups. This information may have strategic value in analyzing patterns and trends, especially if one type of ammunition is turning up in unexpected places.

Exhibit Screening Protocols

The following protocol represents a conglomeration of various common practices and helpful hints for screening and triaging exhibits gathered from a number of IBIS clients around the world.

- Determine the number of firearms involved.

- Screen by caliber, class characteristics, and individual markings, selecting a representative sample of bullets for each of the firearms identified in the screening process.

- Screen by manufacturer of ammunition, bullet design (flat base, boat tail, concave base etc.) and material (lead, copper, brass, nickel, steel etc.).

- If all are from the same manufacturer, bullet design, and material, and are equal in the quality of markings, then one may be chosen for entry into IBIS.

- If more than one manufacturer, bullet design, or material is represented, even if the quality of the markings is equal, consider entering a representative sample for each variation.

- If the bullet bearing surface is damaged, or if the bullet is fragmented, consider entering enough of the damaged or fragmented bullets to equal the number of land engraved areas (LEAs) that would be present on a pristine bullet, or as many LEAs as are available.

- Select a representative sample of cartridge cases for each of the firearms identified in the screening process.

- Screen by manufacturer of ammunition, primer size, design (hemispherical vs. flat etc.), material (brass, nickel, steel etc.), lacquered vs. non-lacquered, and the similarity of marks.

- If all are from the same manufacturer, primer size, design, material, with all lacquered or all non-lacquered, and equal in the quality of markings, then one may be chosen.

- If more than one manufacturer, primer size, design, or material is represented and even if the quality of the markings is equal, consider entering a representative sample for each variation.

- If there is a variation in markings, such as drag marks present on some but not all, or primer flow back present on some but not others, consider entering a representative sample for each variation in the markings.

Critical Elements

- Create an early opportunity for the forensic specialist and the investigator to collaborate and exchange timely and relevant information order to fine-tune and help optimize the remainder of the processes for this critical task.

- Establish a decision matrix against which facts and circumstances can be compared in order to determine the protocols or next steps to be followed for a given case (e.g., additional forensic analysis, scope of correlation, selection of test fire ammunition, crime gun tracing etc.).

Key Considerations

- Exchange the preliminary information between the investigator and the forensic specialist.

- Review the best practices for adoption regarding such items as establishing examination priorities, dealing with multiple pieces of evidence from the same case, communicating preliminary information of value to investigators in a timely manner, and determining the scope of IBIS correlation requests.

Summary

The Most Important Thing: Exchanging information between the investigator and the forensic specialist, in a collaborative manner, early in the examination process to enable the forensic specialist to provide the investigator with preliminary information in a timely manner.

The Next Step: The next chapter discusses the fundamentals of task number seven of *The 13 Critical Tasks*—Test-firing.

Task Seven: Test-firing

Chapter 11

Why Test Fire?

From the *Association of Firearm and Tool Mark Examiners (AFTE) Glossary*, test-firing is "The term used to designate the actual firing of a firearm in a laboratory to obtain representative bullets and cartridge cases for comparison or analysis". Because differences in the hardness, shape, and size of certain ammunition components can impact firearm examination, test-firing becomes an integral part of the automated ballistic identification process. It also helps to ensure the safe collection of the most appropriate exhibits for comparison.

It would be very advantageous to have the test fire ammunition selection criteria in place at the outset of a ballistic identification program, in order to avoid delays in obtaining the best suited ammunition.

In an effort to redistribute workloads, the test fire task can be fairly easily shifted to various suitable locations outside of a lab and can be accomplished by people other than forensic experts. The redistribution of workloads can help prevent bottlenecks and evidence processing delays. Delays are dangerous because it takes longer to identify armed criminals, leaving them free to cause more harm. This problem is compounded by the fact that a gun that is taken into custody by police with no readily apparent connection to a murder or other serious crime will most often fall to the bottom of the lab's case work priority list. Experience has proven that these seemingly insignificant guns can become major factors in breaking a murder case or series of cases wide open. All crime guns that are taken into custody should be test fired in a timely manner in order to keep step with the presumptive approach and the balancing of people, processes, and technology.

Using trained police officers and crime scene technicians outside of the lab environment to test fire guns to obtain bullet and cartridge case test fire samples is a great example of balancing the people part of the three-legged stool. This practice is being done in many places successfully. Removing the test fire workload requirement from the shoulders of the forensic experts working in the lab frees more of their time for conducting examinations.

Establishing a protocol to test fire only certain specified types of guns seized by the police, thereby narrowing the field, is an excellent example of balancing the processes part of the three-legged stool. The criteria should be based on focusing efforts on the types of guns that are most often used in crimes within a particular region. Test-firing only specific types of guns can prevent wasting time and resources on firearms that are unlikely to ever be used in crimes.

Police in Palm Beach County, Florida, have purchased portable test fire bullet trap systems which allow for the safe discharge of a firearm and the collection of the fired ammunition components outside of the lab environment. This is a great example of how to balance the technology part of the three-legged stool.

Recommended Best Practices

Safety First—Maintain a Safe and Uncontaminated Environment

Firearm Safety: Everyone working in a firearm identification unit should be required to attend and pass an accredited firearm safety class. All firearms should be kept with the bolt open, slide back, or cylinder held open with a plastic cable tie or other device to render the firearm inoperable. Firearms should only be loaded at the firing range or in the bullet recovery room. When test-firing, never load more than one cartridge into the magazine, clip or cylinder at a time. Never test fire a firearm alone; be accompanied by an observer. Wear safety glasses when test-firing. The plastic cable tie or other safety device should be replaced before leaving the firing range or bullet recovery room with a firearm. No ammunition, other than evidence, should be allowed at an examiner's workstation. Accidents happen, have a Red Cross approved first aid kit with an assortment of bandages including large sterile pads.

Environmental Safety: All personnel should be vaccinated against hepatitis A, B, and tetanus. All bullets and bullet fragments should be soaked in a bleach and water solution before examination. When examining evidence, always wear plastic gloves and safety glasses. When examining clothing, wear plastic gloves, a respirator, and safety glasses.

Any work dealing with chemicals should be performed under a fuming hood, and a respirator should be worn. All chemicals should be stored in an approved closet. Your work area should be covered with new paper (butcher or wrapping paper). Never eat at your workstation. Never store food in a refrigerator that is used for the storage of evidence. Wash your hands frequently.

A Common Approach to the Selection of Test Fired Ammunition

- If a firearm submitted for examination contained ammunition when it was taken into custody, test fire it using the same brand and type of ammunition.

- If a firearm submitted for examination contained no ammunition when taken into custody, test fire it using the ammunition identified according to an established protocol based on:

    o The makes and types of ammunition most commonly encountered in the legitimate market in the region.

  or

    o The makes and types of ammunition most commonly encountered in crimes in the region. IBIS data can be reviewed to identify ammunition patterns and trends.

- Select a number of ammunition types that are commonly used and found during criminal acts in your area. These will be the test standards.

- Select a number of crime guns that are common in your area and test fire them using the previously identified ammunition.

- From the recovered test fires, visually compare all the samples and narrow the selection to three categories based on the quality of markings left on the fired ammunition components:

    o Category One: should be the ammunition that marks the best.

    o Category Two: should be the ammunition that marks the worst.

o   Category Three: should be the ammunition that marks in between the best and worst.

Note: In a networked system where correlations will occur between one site and another, the various sites should use a test fire protocol that uses the same brands of ammunition. This ensures consistency across sites.

Dealing with Brass and Nickel Primers—
South African Police Service

The South African Police Service reports that they frequently encounter ammunition used in crimes which contains either brass or nickel primers. These types of primers mark differently due to the composition of the different metals. In order to optimize correlation performance when dealing with different ammunition types and materials, this best practice involves a test-firing protocol in which three test fires are taken using three types of ammunition. It establishes a probability as to the boundaries in which most ammunition in the region would fall. The protocol requires that every firearm is test fired using each of the three categories of ammunition.

The NIBIN Protocol—ATF

Select a number of ammunition types that are commonly found in the region of interest and used during criminal acts in the area. Select a number of firearms, test fire them and enter the test fires into the IBIS system. Determine which types of ammunition perform best when processed through the IBIS system.

The NIBIN Squad—Phoenix Police Department

In conjunction with the Crime Lab, the Phoenix Police Department's Violent Crimes Bureau, NIBIN Squad, enters crime scene evidence cartridge cases and test fires into the NIBIN database. Below are some examples of the NIBIN Squad protocols:

- Does the evidence need to be processed for DNA and/or prints, or is a function test necessary? If the answer is "yes", the item(s) must be sent to the Crime lab first. Submit a lab request and also request that the item(s) be entered into NIBIN following the processing for DNA/prints/function test.

- If processing of the item(s) by the Crime Lab is not necessary, submit a request to the NIBIN squad to have the item(s) entered into the NIBIN database.

- Submit all requests for evidence scene casings and test-fires (semi-auto handguns and long guns) to the NIBIN squad requests address in Outlook.

- Complete the NIBIN Request Worksheet word document, save it to your computer and send it as an e-mail attachment.

- The NIBIN detective assigned to your case will make a case management entry and supplement your report when the entry has been completed. After making a request, you will normally not be contacted unless a hit is identified. Contact the assigned NIBIN detective should you have any questions.

- NIBIN Detectives are assigned to work with specific details: Homicide Unit - Property Crimes Bureau North & South - Assaults Unit - Night Detectives - Auto Theft Unit -Document Crimes Unit - Drug Enforcement Bureau - Family Investigations Bureau - Robbery Unit - Gang Enforcement Unit

Open Test Fire "Shoots"—Indiana State Police

The Indiana State Police Ballistics Unit will periodically host "Test fire Shoots" at a local gun range providing police agencies the opportunity to bring their seized firearms to the range and have them test fired according to established protocols, with the assistance of personnel from the State Police Lab.

Security Industry Test Firing (SITF) Program—New South Wales Police Department

In May 2003, police in New South Wales, Australia, began a ballistic testing program for handguns in accordance with legislation requiring the State's private security service agencies (e.g., armed guards and cash couriers) to submit their firearms for testing. The legislation creating the program called the Security Industry Test Firing (SITF) Program was passed in response to what law makers viewed as an alarming and rising trend in crime directed at the security industry. Security agencies were being targeted for the firearms that they possessed as well as for the money they guarded. Criminals had come to view security agencies as a source of handguns, since national restrictions prevented general public access to handguns. The law requires that all security industry handguns be submitted to the New South Wales Police for identification and record keeping. In addition, a sample test fire from each gun is imaged and stored in a database for later cross-checking with ballistic evidence found at crime scenes. IBIS technology is used by the SITF Program for ballistic imaging and comparison. The program has demonstrated that it can track security agency firearms that are used to commit serious crimes, such as armed robbery, assault, and murder, and that it could provide tactical and strategic intelligence of value to deal more effectively with the problem in New South Wales. New South Wales Police have used the SITF Program and IBIS technology to alert them when a security-agency-owned firearm was used in a crime, to track the gun's repeated use without having to wait until it was recovered, and to identify recovered crime guns as stolen security agency firearms despite the fact that the identifying serial numbers had been obliterated. The program has been effective in providing police with unique and valuable information of both a tactical and strategic nature. Tactically, the program helps investigators to combine and leverage the information known about the linked cases in order to develop new leads and advance their investigations. Strategically, the program helps crime analysts to identify patterns and trends associated with the diversion of guns to criminals, so that policy makers can develop new strategies and tactics to combat urban gun violence.

Stolen Firearms Lookout Programs

Some police agencies in a number of countries test fire their own firearms and the firearms of other government agencies. Some agencies, like those in the United States, keep the test fires stored and filed. In the event that a particular firearm is stolen, the test fire is removed from storage and entered into IBIS for tracking. Other countries actually enter the test fires into IBIS at the outset to help detect improper use, theft, and diversion.

Critical Elements

- Establish firearm safety and anti-contamination protocols for test-firing.

- Establish ammunition selection protocols for test-firing.

- Ensure that a timely and sustainable process is in place for making the test-firing of guns seized by police a priority, including those that have no readily apparent connection to a murder or other serious crime.

Key Considerations

- Prepare for the execution of the test fire protocols well in advance (identify and procure test-firing supplies and bullet trap systems etc.).

- Avoid delays and backlogs—consider redistributing workloads to help maintain priorities by balancing people, processes, and technology.

- Communicate the protocols and provide the required training.

Summary

The Most Important Thing: Establishing a process to ensure the safe collection of test fired exhibits and to select ammunition materials which can optimize the IBIS automated correlation process.

The Next Step: The test fire process is a critical to linking a seized firearm to a crime or series of crimes. The next step is to acquire an IBIS image. The next chapter discusses the fundamentals of task number eight of *The 13 Critical Tasks*—Acquiring Images of Fired Ammunition Components.

12
Chapter

Task Eight: Acquiring Images of Fired Ammunition Components

Why Image Evidence?

Police forces today must deal with rising tides of urban gun violence while resources dwindle and unprecedented service demands are made by the public. Governments need and want the most advanced technology available to achieve increases in productivity at reasonable operating costs.

From its inception over 90 years ago, the use of forensic ballistics to help solve crimes has been essentially a two-dimensional process. Forensic experts peering through their comparison microscopes have always known that they were viewing objects which were three-dimensional in nature.

Recent scientific studies[15] indicate that three-dimensional imaging is the key to making significant improvements in the field of forensic ballistics. Forensic Technology shares the same view and also believes that the strengths of both 2D and 3D must be combined to produce the best solution possible.

Therefore, Forensic Technology has responded to the needs of law enforcers worldwide by developing IBIS (Integrated Ballistics Identification System). The latest generation of products, IBIS TRAX-3D, offers a highly automated and comprehensive way of imaging ballistics in both two and three dimensions.

The technology behind the IBIS TRAX-3D product family is a generation beyond that of the earlier **IBIS®** Heritage™ 2D products. IBIS TRAX-3D provides higher-quality 2D images and introduces 3D capabilities, more automation, and powerful analysis tools. It is also able

---

[15] Journal of Forensic Sciences, American Academy of Forensic Sciences, May 2008, Vol. 53, No. 3.

to integrate with the existing IBIS Heritage network, ensuring a seamless transition and maintaining high levels of efficiency and effectiveness. Data sharing and cross-comparison is made possible because both product families use standard configurations and methods to capture 2D images. This backward compatibility is imperative for IBIS Heritage users who have invested a great deal of time and effort in building a national crime solving resource of ballistic information.

IBIS TRAX-3D's architecture uses a more modular approach than that of IBIS Heritage. IBIS TRAX-3D divides the major operations into three general areas of data processing: collection, storage and comparison, and analysis and reporting.

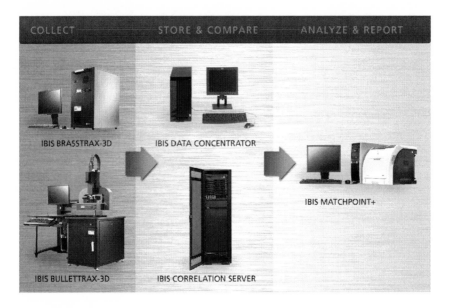

In addition to allowing more-flexible deployment options, this approach overcomes some of the productivity limitations and technical compromises associated with a single platform configuration.

Because of the high degree of automation, users of IBIS TRAX-3D image acquisition systems require little training to consistently collect high quality data. In fact, **IBIS® BRASSTRAX-3D™** can be used inside or outside a laboratory and can be operated by people other than expert firearm examiners. Therefore, ballistic evidence collection workloads for IBIS networks can be better balanced—the firearm examiners can then be free to focus on work requiring their expert skills. This not only reduces processing time, but increases productivity.

The high level of automation in IBIS TRAX-3D systems makes it easier to use and ensures consistent levels of high quality data collection. It also increases productivity and cost effectiveness by facilitating multitasking and reducing the skill level and associated training requirements. Machine automation reduces operator variance in data collection. On the input side, it promotes uniformity and standardization; on the output side, it produces optimal comparison results. The acquisition process automatically initiates and controls parameters such as lighting, focus, and outlining. It takes only a few minutes to set up a bullet or a cartridge case, and once started, the actual image acquisition process is fully automated freeing up the operator for other tasks.

In taking the presumptive approach to the investigation of crimes involving the misuse of firearms, good quality image data must be collected from fired bullet and cartridge case specimens in both two and three dimensions in order for the best possible data to be extracted from the automated ballistic imaging process. Its high quality 2D and 3D imaging capacity, automated processing features, and modular architecture make IBIS TRAX-3D particularly valuable in facilitating the design of new and innovative work processes to break free from traditional boundaries, extend the reach and range of the technology, redirect workloads, and help reduce case backlogs.

Recommended Best Practices

Proficiency Testing

Administered at the lab site, proficiency testing is sometimes done one month after the completion of the Forensic Technology (FT) Basic User course. If a user fails, FT recommends that the user work with a mentor for a period of one month before retaking the test. A proficiency test should be administered once a year to all users of FT products in order to realize the following benefits:

- Standard image quality throughout the network

- Adherence to acquisition protocols

- Confirmation to section supervisors and lab directors regarding personnel efficiency

- Satisfaction to operators after having been certified by a world recognized company

Routine Review of IBIS Images and Case Information

A best practice is to establish a quality control log as part of the quality program and maintain it in the IBIS work area. Any time during a quality review session that a case or exhibit is identified as containing an error, it should be logged and the corrections made and noted. The review should include both image quality (such as focus, lighting, delimiter placement, etc.) and case information (such as date, crime, and location). While performing IBIS result review and image comparisons, operators may encounter errors relative to a case or exhibit that should be noted in the log for quality follow-up and correction. Continuous follow-up and reinforcement by an assigned site administrator can be an effective means of quality control.

Bracketing

The quality of the markings left on a fired ammunition components is of major importance to the firearm examiner and the ballistic imaging systems. Sometimes the differences in marks on fired components discharged from the same gun can be so great as to preclude a comparative determination. Bracketing tries to overcome this by relying upon the consideration of multiple test fires and pieces of evidence fired from the same gun to account for the normal variations in marks inherent to the science. For example, consider that the quality of marks on test fires could be ranked from one to ten with ten being the best. IBIS bracketing would involve selecting two exhibits fired from the same gun for system entry—one at low end of the scale of poor marks and one at the high end of the scale with good marks. This in effect creates a virtual "bracket" in the database, from 1 to 10, against which new exhibits can be ranked. For example, a test fire with marks ranked in the middle of the scale will be ranked a 5 when searched against the database. Note, however, that bracketing can have workload and system operation tradeoffs if overused.

IBIS FastTRAX

FastTRAX, the IBIS data entry and review services provided by Forensic Technology, employs its own highly trained and skilled personnel to perform the imaging of fired ammunition components and the IBIS database correlation results review.

Forensic Technology Training Standards

Designed with specific law enforcement needs in mind, the Forensic Technology training department identifies customers' requirements in order to create task-based training guides that shorten the learning curve and immerse users in the software's workflow so that they can work sooner and more efficiently. A Subject Matter Expert (SME) works closely within the FT training team, and it is the ongoing responsibility of this SME to ensure the technical knowledge of the trainers delivering information in the FT classroom. A series of tools is designed for each curriculum: pre-assessment, course plan, training guide, and post-assessment. A member of the training team can also visit a client to perform the following tasks on-site: interview users to determine their roles vis-a-vis the software; learn how training can be more beneficial or in-line with their needs; present possible documentation and training alternatives; observe training and share relevant observations with the design team.

Critical Elements

- Training: Get the proper IBIS training. Proficiency is critical. The worst possible scenario for the user and the technology provider is to not realize success with IBIS because of improper image acquisition.

- Quality assurance: Implement a quality assurance protocol to monitor the input of both image and case-related data.

- Continued adherence to protocols: Follow the IBIS protocols that are taught during IBIS training; they are designed to maximize the advantages of the system. For example, the system enables the capturing of three different types of marks from the surface of fired cartridge cases. All three should be captured in order to optimize the correlation process.

Key Considerations

- Identify who will be acquiring images and the required skill level. For example, consider these three levels of operators:

  o Basic Operator: Just about anyone with basic office computer skills can be trained in a matter of days to perform the data input, including image acquisition of a fired cartridge case and bullet representing a single test fire exhibit or single piece of evidence. A basic operator can work independently, with general supervision, inside a lab or remotely from another location (e.g., a police department), entering single test fire exhibits and criminal case data involving a single piece of ballistic evidence (i.e., one fired bullet or one fired cartridge case). A basic operator is normally not trained or expected to enter criminal case data involving multiple pieces of ballistic evidence which must be triaged in an effort to select only one or two exhibits for actual data input.

  o IBIS Technician: In addition to the requirements of a basic operator, an IBIS technician will have additional training and experience (a matter of a few weeks) providing him or her with the ability to discriminate between multiple pieces of criminal case evidence which must be triaged to select one or two exhibits for data input.

  o Firearm Examiner: The requirements for a firearm examiner go well beyond those of a basic operator or IBIS technician. A firearm examiner will have sufficient levels of in-depth training and practical experience (generally two to three years at a minimum) in all areas of firearm examination and forensic ballistics to be recognized and accepted by a court of law as an expert witness.

- Establish training plans for various operator levels. Also, consider safety and environmental issues.

- Establish proficiency standards and testing procedures.

- Establish and integrate quality assurance standards and methods to monitor the input of data.

- Post training aids (such as image acquisition standards charts) for user-ready reference.

Summary

The Most Important Thing: Collecting good quality image data from fired bullet and cartridge case specimens in both two and three dimensions so that the best data possible is generated from the automated ballistic imaging process.

The Next Step: With the input of quality data addressed here, the next chapter discusses the fundamentals of task number nine of *The 13 Critical Tasks*—Reviewing Correlation Results.

13
Chapter

Task Nine: Reviewing Correlation Results

Why Review Correlation Results?

The goal of reviewing the correlation results generated by the **IBIS®** Correlation Server is to find high confidence matches among the various images of fired ammunition components stored in the IBIS database. The identification of prospective matches can, in turn, help generate substantial crime solving leads and provide prevention value when taking the presumptive approach described in this book. This value should more than justify the investment of time and resources that are required when executing the IBIS component of any crime solving program.

Correlation results review represents a crucial deliverable at a critical juncture. Careful attention must be given to this task and its various elements because if a match is missed here, a second opportunity to find it may not present itself.

How to Review Correlation Results

It may be worth taking some time here to clarify how prospective matches and hits are found between ballistic evidence and test fires in an automated ballistic technology environment like IBIS.

Firstly, the technology generates information which can be used to readily find the prospective matches; it does not identify matches between ballistic exhibits. A firearm examiner uses the reported information to select potentially matching exhibits and then compares them physically under a comparison microscope in order to render an expert opinion. In his or her opinion, if a match is confirmed between two cases, a "hit" is declared. The value of the IBIS correlation process is that it can perform thousands of comparisons in a matter of minutes at speeds well beyond human capability.

Secondly, this computing power allows firearm examiners to do what had previously been extremely difficult to sustain—conduct a reasonably accurate review of every piece of evidence against every other piece in the inventory (IBIS database). When the IBIS systems are linked in a network, the inventory of one system, in effect, becomes the inventory of all systems, giving the users the ability to do what had previously been impossible to perform and sustain.

Correlation results are examined using **IBIS®** MATCHPOINT+™—the expert's analysis station for reviewing the prospective matches returned by the IBIS Correlation Server.

MATCHPOINT+ empowers the firearm examiner to virtually emulate the functions of a comparison microscope, such as the image orientation, the adjustment of the magnification, and the direction of the light source. The unique 3D capabilities also provide new possibilities beyond the microscope experience by allowing experts to better visualize images of all types of cartridge cases and bullets, from the pristine to the most severely damaged—including bullets fired through polygonal rifled barrels and many smooth bore or converted firearms. MATCHPOINT+ provides quantitative data to enhance confidence in findings today, and precision measurements to enhance confidence in the scientific basis of the process tomorrow.

MATCHPOINT+ can help reduce the wait time and lineups that can occur when sharing a single comparison microscope in the lab—as experts will need to spend less time there.

As previously discussed, Forensic Technology believes that 2D is good and that 3D is better, but 2D plus 3D is best. This is exactly what IBIS TRAX-3D technology provides to help firearm examiners see more, know more, and link more.

By combining 2D and 3D data, the 2D texture can be overlaid over the rendered 3D model using an adjustable simulated light source, for superior visualization. This combination allows for the dynamic observation of the surface information by adjusting the mix of 2D texture and 3D topography.

Some forensic experts who have had the opportunity to use MATCHPOINT+ to make comparisons of **IBIS®** BULLETTRAX-3D™ images have commented that the traditional comparison microscope may well become redundant in the future because of the state-of-the-art visualization capabilities made possible by 3D technology and high-definition systems like IBIS TRAX-3D. Furthermore, 3D comparisons can help match bullet pairs that are challenging when using 2D images or a comparison microscope. This is especially true when comparing bullets with different material compositions, such as when comparing lead bullets against copper-jacketed bullets.

Bullet Analysis Capabilities and Tools

Adjustable 2D/3D Rendering

Adjusting the level of rendering between 2D and 3D leverages the strengths of both for the optimal viewing of surface marks. The 2D image of the bullet surface is enhanced by being applied to the 3D topographical model which reveals useful mark information.

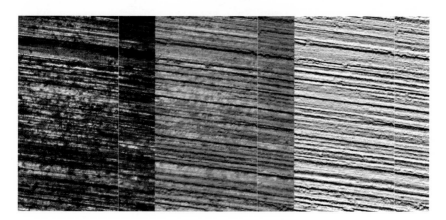

Bullet MultiViewer

The Bullet MultiViewer allows for the high-level comparison of potential matching candidates with the complete view of the bullet's circumference.

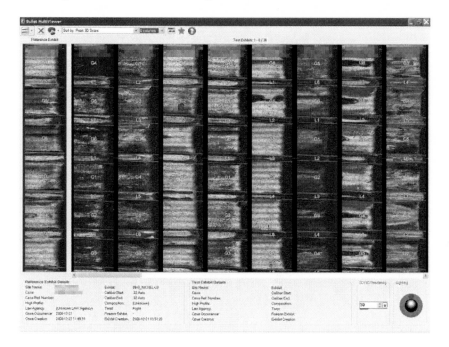

Bullet Side-by-Side Viewer

The Bullet Side-by-Side Viewer allows for the in-depth comparison of two bullets, similar to the experience when using a comparison microscope. Many controls and tools are available to assist in making conclusions, such as dynamic lighting and 3D rendering.

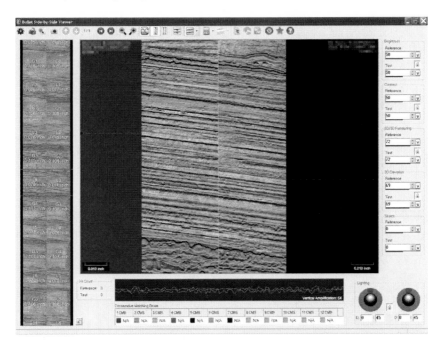

Profile

The bullet profile is a powerful tool that is based on quantitative information of the bullet surface—never before available to the firearm examiner. The two bullet surface cross sections can be visually compared. The more similar the two profiles are, the more likely it is that the two exhibits match.

Vertical Amplification: 5X

Rulers

Rulers can be applied to measure distances on a bullet's surface: the lateral, vertical, and depth differences as well as the total distance between two points on the bullet surface.

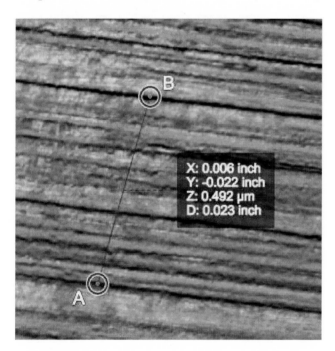

X: 0.006 inch
Y: -0.022 inch
Z: 0.492 µm
D: 0.023 inch

Automated Identification of Consecutive Matching Striae (CMS) on Bullets

CMS is a scientific approach whose goal is to objectively count groups of matching striae to determine similarity between bullets. The high-definition of 3D bullet images offers accurate length, width, and depth information about the bullet's surface topography, thus enabling MATCHPOINT+ to objectively identify groups of consecutive matching striae (CMS). Microscopic 3D measurements of the surface topography allow for the exploration of new scientific methods, such as CMS, to support analytical conclusions.

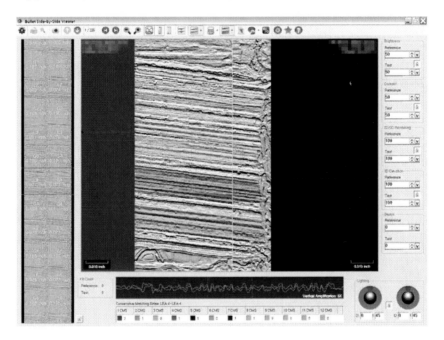

Cartridge Case Analysis Capabilities and Tools

Adjustable 2D/3D Rendering of Primer Image

Adjusting the level of rendering between 2D and 3D leverages the strengths of both for optimal viewing of surface marks. The 2D image of the breech face and firing pin impressions is enhanced by being applied to the 3D topographical model which reveals useful shape and mark information.

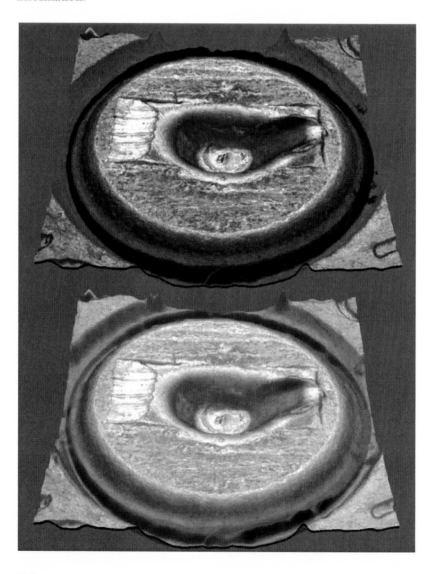

Cartridge Case MultiViewer

The Cartridge Case MultiViewer allows for the high-level comparison of potential matching candidates with a simultaneous view of multiple cartridge case images.

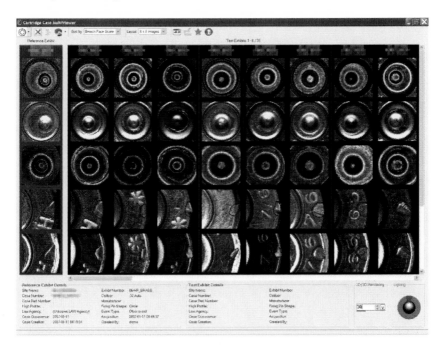

Cartridge Case Side-by-Side Viewer

The Cartridge Case Side-by-Side Viewer allows for the in-depth comparison of two cartridge cases, similar to the experience when using a comparison microscope. Many controls and tools are available to assist in making conclusions, such as dynamic lighting, 3D rendering and primer 3D reverse view.

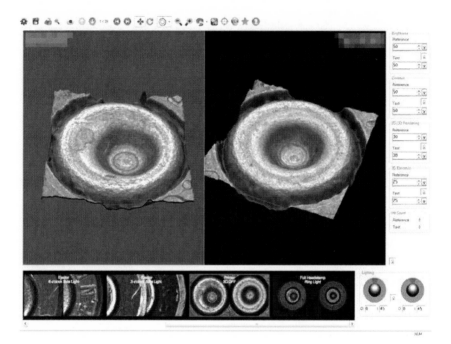

Full Headstamp Image

The complete cartridge case headstamp is captured, potentially giving access to additional marks that are not included in other acquired images. This image can be used as a record of the exhibit without having the physical cartridge case in hand. It is useful for quality control and validation by observing the relative position of the markings and showing caliber and manufacturer information, if present.

Primer 3D Reverse Visualization

The 3D model of the cartridge case primer can be rotated to view the firing pin impression from the underside. This new perspective is unique to the IBIS TRAX-3D technology and is a key differentiator from modern comparison microscopes and other ballistic analysis systems. This feature in MATCHPOINT+ can be used to quickly discern differences between exhibits. For example, when comparing the profile of firing pin impressions, using this feature can sometimes help differentiate firearm types based on the typical characteristics of the firing pin used in the manufacture of different firearm models. Below, the distinct shapes of two different firing pins are evident.

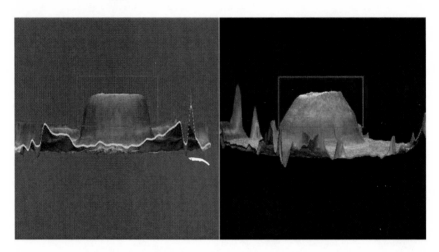

Cartridge Case Primer 3D All-In-Focus Image

This useful visualization mode allows the analysis of the complete primer area with every point in perfect focus on a single image. This improves the likelihood of finding relevant marks. For example, the figure below is a side-by-side comparison of two Makarov cartridge cases showing the breech face and firing pin impressions. The colored rectangles highlight seven visible areas of similarity. This information could prompt an examiner to continue the examination and consider all available marks in order to increase the probability of making a match.

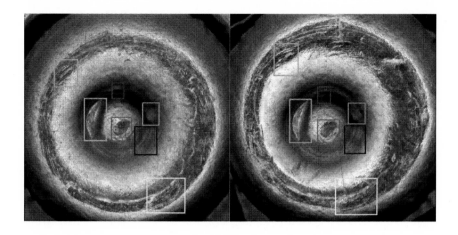

Correlation Results Filtering, Printing, and Reporting

Multiple correlation scores can be sorted and analyzed in a graphical view to easily distinguish gaps in the scores, thus enabling operators to expedite their analysis. MATCHPOINT+ is equipped with a color printer to print reports, information screens, viewer screens, and images for presentation purposes.

Recommended Best Practices

The IBIS Protocol

Forensic Technology recommends the review of the exhibits for the top 10 prospective matches returned and ranked by the IBIS Correlation Server. One of IBIS's strengths is that it processes the images of three distinct markings that can be used to help identify possible matches. Each of the marks are captured independently of one another and tests have shown that capturing and evaluating all available marks significantly increases the chances of a making a match. Some types of firearms do not leave quality breech face or firing pin marks; however, they do leave quality ejector marks. One such firearm is the AK-47. For this type of weapon, the ejector mark is often the most reliable mark for evaluations. A firearm examiner evaluates a number of marks to help determine that two exhibits were fired from the same gun.

Expand the Search Beyond the Top Ten

IBIS operators are not limited to reviewing only the top ten results. If time and workloads permit, operators should look further down the list of correlation results in order to find potential hits. Forensic Technology's scientists indicate that match probabilities drop fairly rapidly among correlation results ranked below the top ten. Although the IBIS algorithms are tuned to rank samples as high as possible on the list, some matching exhibits will fall below the top ten rankings for a number of reasons related to people, processes, and technology. Therefore, some IBIS user sites review more than the top ten results (e.g., the top 25) as a matter of protocol. Others use a flexible protocol which, depending on the case at hand, allows for the review of exhibits even further down the list.

New York City Police Department and South African Police Service (SAPS) Review Specialists

The New York City Police Department (NYPD) and the South African Police Service (SAPS) assign Ballistics Unit staff that are exclusively dedicated to the review of IBIS correlation results. These specialists become very skilled at finding potential matches and are one of the reasons that NYPD and SAPS are the two leading IBIS users in the world in terms of the number of cases linked or hits generated.

Outsourcing Correlation Reviews

Services such as FastTRAX, the IBIS data entry and review services provided by Forensic Technology, employs its own highly-trained and skilled personnel to perform the imaging of fired ammunition components and the IBIS correlation results review.

Critical Elements

- Training: Acquire the skills required to interpret the IBIS correlation results and utilize the various MATCHPOINT+ analysis tools.

- Quality assurance: Implement a quality assurance protocol to evaluate all of the output data, such as the correlation results for breech face impressions, firing pin impressions, and ejector marks, and other case information as well.

- Continued adherence to protocols: Enforce a protocol to ensure that the correlation results review is conducted for every exhibit reported and that it is completed in a timely manner which meets the needs of the investigative and prosecutorial stakeholders.

Key Considerations

- Identify the persons responsible for conducting IBIS correlation results reviews.

- Create a comprehensive correlation results review protocol.

- Identify quality assurance methods for the correlation results review process.

Summary

The Most Important Thing: Reviewing IBIS correlation results in a timely and skillful manner is crucial at this critical juncture so as not to miss potential matches.

The Next Step: After a prospective IBIS match has been identified, it must be confirmed by a qualified firearm examiner. The next chapter discusses the fundamentals of task number ten of *The 13 Critical Tasks*— Confirming Hits.

14
Chapter

Task Ten: Confirming Hits

Why Search for Hits?

A program based on the presumptive approach depends on people. Although technology helps people be more efficient and effective, and supports previously unsustainable operations, the confirmation of prospective matches is dependent upon trained and qualified personnel. As described earlier, the confirmation of a match made between two cases is called a "hit".

ATF defines a "hit" as "the linkage of two different crime investigations by the user of the NIBIN (IBIS) technology, where previously there had been no known connection between the investigations".

Today, the actual confirmation of the potential matches is done by experts using a traditional comparison microscope. Depending on the characteristics of the exhibits under examination and the adjustments required by the microscope, an examiner may experience difficulty in finding the corresponding areas of agreement between the markings on each exhibit. These difficulties can significantly increase the amount of time and effort required for the examination and can affect the eventual conclusion.

New technology that takes advantage of 2D and 3D visualization tools, such as MATCHPOINT+, system can help firearm examiners to make comparative conclusions using a comparison microscope faster and with less effort.

Automated ballistic identification technology like IBIS also enables agencies to share electronic data at the local, national, regional, and international levels. An agency can now electronically query the evidence inventory of another agency to locate possible matches and hits between cases. This electronic pooling of evidence requires well-coordinated actions between the people who must confirm the cases as hits and the people in possession of the actual evidence that is needed for the confirmation process.

The exchange of evidence immediately raises many issues and is something that requires much thought and deliberation. The retrieval of physical evidence is a common obstacle and can be a source of frustration and delay. Whatever solutions are established, they must be executed accurately and in a timely manner so as not to become stumbling blocks to the success of the ballistic data sharing program. Forensic Technology is currently researching other ways of exchanging ballistic data in a more efficient and effective manner.

Recommended Best Practices

The ATF National Firearm Examiner Training Academy

The National Firearm Examiner Training Academy provides training for apprentice/entry-level firearm and tool mark examiners from federal, state, and local law enforcement agencies. The Academy curriculum is composed of the fundamentals of firearm and tool mark examinations and serves as a basis for the trainee, under supervision, to develop into a qualified firearm and tool mark examiner. Applications for this training are accepted from law enforcement laboratories. Portions of this training are held at the ATF National Laboratory Center in Ammendale, Maryland. There is no cost for the training; however, students and/or their home agencies are responsible for certain travel related expenses. For more information, go to www.atf.gov/training/firearms.

ATF NIBIN Hit Definition and Protocol

A "hit" is linkage of two different crime investigations by the user of the NIBIN technology, where previously there had been no known connection between the investigations. A hit is a linkage between cases, not individual pieces of evidence. Multiple bullets and/or casings may be entered as part of the same case record; in this event, each discovered linkage to an additional case constitutes a hit. A hit must be confirmed by a firearm examiner examining the actual specimens under a microscope. Other NIBIN linkages derived by investigative leads, hunches, or previously identified laboratory examinations, are not "hits" according to this definition. Therefore, other linkages previously termed "warm hits" should not be counted as hits. When an inter-agency hit occurs, the agency initiating and confirming the microscopic comparison will be credited for the hit.

Marking Hits in the IBIS System: Hits meeting the definition above should be linked in the IBIS system, using the procedures provided in instructional materials from Forensic Technology (FT). Remember that if a link is confirmed between two cases, it is necessary to note this in each IBIS case record. Linkages derived by investigative leads, hunches, or previously identified laboratory examinations should only be noted in the comments section of the IBIS screen. These linkages are not to be designated as hits. When an inter-agency hit is confirmed, each involved site should mark the hit in IBIS, using procedures provided in instructional materials from FT.

Statistical Reporting: For inter-agency hits, only the agency initiating and confirming the comparison should include the hit in its statistics reported to ATF NIBIN.

Open Case File—Allegheny County Medical Examiner

The Allegheny County Medical Examiner's lab provides forensic services for a number of law enforcement agencies within the county. The agreement with submitters of ballistic evidence is that the evidence will be retained by the lab until such time as the case is disposed of or the submitting agency instructs otherwise. This practice is designed to eliminate the need for time- and resource-wasting callbacks of evidence. For example, the practice in many areas of the country is to summit fired bullets and evidence to the lab. The lab will examine and process the evidence through IBIS and network like NIBIN and, if there is no further need to hold on to the evidence, it is returned to the submitting agency. Subsequently, new evidence is submitted by the same agency or another agency, or a gun is sent in for test-firing and processing through IBIS. When the new evidence or test fires are processed through IBIS, it frequently happens that the new evidence or test fires appear to have similarities to the evidence that was previously submitted and then returned. Now, the lab has to issue a callback for this prior evidence to be returned for comparison with new evidence. This callback procedure takes time and resources on the part of the lab and the police agency. It has been reported during *The 13 Critical Tasks Workshops* that the callback process could take anywhere from days to weeks to months and that it is not unusual for the same evidence to be called back multiple times. Not only do callbacks waste time and resources, they expose the evidence to loss and damage and can leave its integrity in question. Maintaining an open case file of the evidence on behalf of the submitting agency until it is no longer needed avoids these pitfalls.

Centralization of Evidence—NYPD

The New York City Police Department has a policy in which all firearms and firearm related evidence is sent to a single centralized ballistics unit for examination, entry into IBIS, and gun tracing. The NYPD has established partnership agreements with other federal, state, and local law enforcement agencies operating within the jurisdiction of the city to submit all of their firearms and firearm related evidence to the NYPD Ballistics Unit.

Critical Elements

- Employ trained and qualified firearm examiners who can confirm matches and declare hits.

- Ensure that physical evidence can be retrieved from its storage location in a timely manner and in accordance with chain of custody protocols and established laboratory intake processes.

- Report the results of examinations.

Key Considerations

- Define the terms for prospective matches, confirmed matches (hits) and links between cases.

- Define the protocol for the retrieval of firearms and firearm related evidence for examination at the lab.

- Define the protocol for confirming matches and exchanging data about evidence and test fires between different jurisdictions.

Summary

The Most Important Thing: Trained and qualified personnel confirming prospective matches (i.e., declare "hits") and providing detectives with more-timely investigative leads.

<u>The Next Step:</u> With a hit declared, the stakeholders need to know. The next chapter discusses the fundamentals of task number eleven of *The 13 Critical Tasks*—Communicating Hit Information.

15
Chapter

Task Eleven: Communicating Hit Information

Why Communicate?

Like any other asset, information can be extremely valuable if used wisely and is virtually worthless if squandered or ignored. The introduction of automated ballistic identification technology almost 20 years ago created a new dynamic in the way in which information about guns and crimes could be gathered and shared.

The reality for well over half a century was that information about guns and their connection to crimes was generally obtained in reaction to a request made by police to conduct a particular examination. For several decades, this mind-set prevailed from one generation of law enforcers to the next and still exists in many places today.

The 13 Critical Tasks

Today, firearm examiners, using automated ballistic identification technology like IBIS, are likely to uncover information about links between crimes, guns, and suspects in the lab at their workstations. They will commonly encounter the information before the investigating detectives do.

However, just like in a relay race, forensic personnel must pass the "information baton" to the investigators in a timely manner.

Additionally, the investigators must be aware that information of this nature can be generated, they must appreciate its value, and they must understand what must be done with it.

Protocols need to be established to ensure that the information is communicated quickly and appropriately pursued, and that crime-solving opportunities are not missed.

Automated ballistic identification technology, when applied according to the presumptive approach, changes the prevailing dynamic and puts the ballistics lab in a position to be much more proactive when obtaining information about guns and their connection to crimes. Most importantly, the ballistics technology helps the lab to sustain this position.

You know that there is a communication problem when you hear statements like those listed below from the forensic specialists in the lab...

- "We don't know if we are getting all of the evidence that is being recovered at crime scenes, nor do we know if we are getting all the guns that are taken into police custody."

- "I called the detective assigned to the case and told him that we made a hit between his case and a gun recovered in another case. He asked me what a hit was. When I told him he answered—OK, so what? He didn't seem interested at all."

- "We never get feedback from the detectives about the value of the hits that we refer to them—we are left in the dark and are questioning why we are putting continued efforts into this program."

- "We don't know who the investigating detectives are—their names are not on the evidence transmittal forms because they change all the time, so we never know if the right people are getting the hit information that we generate."

...or when you hear statements like these from the detectives:

- "I didn't know the Lab could do that—this is great stuff—how long have we been able to do this? I wish they had told us sooner."

- "We never collect the spent cartridge cases—we usually just kick them off the street into the gutter."

- "When we send guns or evidence to the lab, we never hear anything back, or if we do, it's months or sometimes years later."

- "The detective assigned to the case never sees the hit referral reports—they all go to another unit and sit on somebody's desk for months."

- "I have never seen a hit report."

- "All of a sudden we started getting these hit reports—nobody ever said what we were expected to do with them."

These statements represent commonly recurring remarks made by actual detectives and forensic specialists all over the world.

Three phases of communication are needed when employing the presumptive approach: (1) the relaying of hit information to investigators, (2) the investigative follow-up of the information referred, and (3) the assessment of the value of information referred with regard to advancing the investigation.

While there are many stages along the "13 critical tasks" process in which things may go awry, it is at this stage where communication mishaps and inefficiencies can quickly become labeled as "government waste". Why? Because what is communicated or not communicated at this stage will affect both the reality and the perception of the outcome value of all of the inputs made thus far in terms of people, processes, and technology while taking the presumptive approach.

Attention to this task will help ensure that the program is producing the intended value and will identify a communication problem so that proper remedial actions can be taken.

Taking the time up-front to communicate with investigators about what they can expect to see in a hit report, the potential value of that information, and the expectations of how it is to be handled and reported, can go a long way in ensuring the effectiveness of the entire program.

The documentation and appropriate communication of the investigative follow-up on a hit will help ensure that the information produced in talking the presumptive approach is not wasted and will help administrators gauge the outcome value of the efforts applied. Most will agree that a program that provides no value should not be sustained. However, it would be terrible to withdraw support from a valuable public safety program because efforts were not made to communicate its value to the affected stakeholders—especially those who authorized it and the public who benefits the most from it.

Recommended Best Practices

The Boston Police E-mail Notification System

The Boston Police created an e-mail notification process to communicate hit information. They created a group e-mail protocol based on two groups of people within the police department; those who have a *Need to Know* (NTK) the information and those who *Want to Know* (WTK) the information (as dictated by department protocols). The NTK group includes assigned detectives and supervisors, intelligence and command staff, including the Commissioner. The WTK group includes other approved departmental stakeholders. Currently, about 39 people within the police department are notified of each IBIS hit. The e-mail contains detailed information about the evidence and guns, the people involved, the two or more cases connected by the hit, and the requirements for investigative follow-up.

Note: The Homicide Division is provided with a direct pre-notification, before anyone else in the event that operational security concerns dictate that the information not be shared at that time.

The Boston Police Department Policy for the Follow-up of IBIS Hits

The Boston Police have a policy that requires reporting on leads resulting from an IBIS hit. A detective in charge of investigating a shooting has the responsibility to note any further leads that were a result of an IBIS match. The policy requires reporting every 30 days. The information is entered into the Detective Case Management system.

The New York Police Department Protocol for the Follow-up of Ballistics Computerization Hits

The NYPD Firearms Unit sends follow-up surveys to recipients of hits generated from automated ballistic computer systems. These surveys collect information from the investigators about their follow-up of any leads generated by the hit data. The survey data is electronically managed in a database. Examples of the follow-up actions noted on the survey form are:

- Arrest/additional arrest made

- Substantial lead developed

- Closed investigation re-opened

- Information incorporated into ongoing investigation

- Suspect(s) arrested before information received

- Suspect died before information received

- No investigative leads/investigation closed

The NIBIN Squad—Phoenix Police Department

The NIBIN Squad enters crime scene cartridge cases and test fires into the NIBIN database in conjunction with the Crime Lab of the Phoenix Police Department's Violent Crimes Bureau. NIBIN detectives are assigned to particular investigative units and cases and are tasked with communicating and reporting on NIBIN hits.

Critical Elements

- Collaborate with affected stakeholders on the development and implementation of efficient processes to generate information linking crimes, guns, and suspects. Everyone should know what to expect and what is expected.

- Communicate the information to investigators in a timely manner.

- Create awareness of the process, its value, and the expectations of the stakeholders.

- Require the investigative follow-up of hits.

- Report on the investigative action and hit value.

- Track hits and report them to stakeholders.

Key Considerations

- Employ sustainable methods for communicating the hit information.

- Report on investigative follow-up.

- Create awareness among affected stakeholders.

Summary

<u>The Most Important Thing</u>: Establishing protocols to ensure that hit information is communicated to investigators in a timely manner, that the hits are appropriately pursued, and that crime-solving opportunities are not squandered.

<u>The Next Step:</u> The next chapter discusses the fundamentals of task number twelve of *The 13 Critical Tasks*—Leveraging Tactics and Strategies.

16
Chapter

Task Twelve: Leveraging Tactics and Strategies

Why Leverage?

Just as it is important for programs to be integrated and leveraged, so too must tactics and strategies. In order to ensure that the actions of all stakeholders are optimized, organizational stovepipes must be overcome through the sharing and integration of relevant tactics and strategies. Hit information must be shared and leveraged using the data generated by other strategies. By combining the various types of data gathered in taking the presumptive approach, we can optimize opportunities to generate new and better intelligence, design more effective enforcement tactics, and maximize the outcome value of the entire firearm crime reduction initiative.

For example, tactical benefits can be maximized by leveraging IBIS data, crime gun trace data, and other crime data (e.g., residence of persons with outstanding arrest warrants) as well. Crime mapping and analysis tools can be of great value in increasing the leverage and sustaining the effort.

A good example of maximizing strategic benefits to deliver more outcome value is the Boston Case Study on Freddy Cardoza used in an earlier chapter. Cardoza, a violent criminal, had received a lengthy prison term which removed him from the community upon which he and his fellow gangsters preyed. The presumptive approach delivered tactical benefits that lead to Cardoza's arrest and conviction, and strategic benefits that resulted in Cardoza's removal from the community for a lengthy period of time. Despite what appeared to be a significant outcome value in the Cardoza case, the stakeholders pushed it a step further. Through their continued collaboration on trying to find ways to derive even more value from their work, they developed a strategy that enabled them to use the Cardoza case as a deterrent. Posters and communications about the lengthy sentence received for possessing a single bullet were launched to dissuade younger members of the community from following in Cardoza's footsteps. An effective violence prevention strategy is priceless.

Recommended Best Practices

Project Safe Neighborhoods (PSN)

Project Safe Neighborhoods, mentioned in detail in earlier chapters, is a program administered by the United States Department of Justice (DOJ), focused on reducing gun and gang violence. The program uses collaborative stakeholder planning and execution, the leveraging and integration of programs, communication and outreach, and holding people accountable. PSN marries enforcement with prevention and deterrence efforts. It also adds another very important element that is critical for success: **the resources to help get the job done.** PSN helps provide the participating stakeholders with the tools they need in terms of people, processes, and technology. More information can be found on the Project Safe Neighborhoods Web site: www.psn.gov.

Boston's Impact Players and Street Shootings Review (IPSSR)

As mentioned in earlier chapters, the IPSSR originated out of the Boston Gun Project: Operation Ceasefire, upon which many of the tenets of Project Safe Neighborhood's are built. The programs are based on collaborative partnerships, the integrating of data from the programs of various law enforcement and criminal justice agencies, and the leveraging of grassroots organizations and the faith community.

Pittsburgh Police Department—Mapping and Analyzing NIBIN Hit Data and LIMS Data

The Pittsburgh Police Intelligence Unit imports NIBIN hit data and leverages it with data from the lab's Laboratory Information Management System (LIMS) for trend and pattern analysis using software called Analyst Notebook.

Regional Crime Gun Centers—ATF

ATF has established the Regional Crime Gun Centers (RCGC) concept to ensure 100 percent comprehensive tracing of all recovered crime guns. The purpose of the RCGC is to analyze patterns and trends on a local level that can be detected through comprehensive trace information on recovered crime guns. Equipped with the best technological hardware and research software available, the RCGC is staffed with ATF personnel as well as state and local investigators and analysts who analyze patterns and trends, develop investigative leads to stop the flow of crime guns into the communities, and assist the state and local police departments in the allocation of their resources.

Fusion Centers

According to the United States Department of Justice, a fusion center is "an effective and efficient mechanism to exchange information and intelligence, maximize resources, streamline operations, and improve the ability to fight crime and terrorism by merging data from a variety of sources". For complete guidelines on developing and operating Fusion Centers, go to www.it.ojp.gov/fusioncenter.

Mandated Post Arrest Interviews

Some law enforcement agencies mandate attempts at conducting lawful post arrest interviews of suspects arrested for firearm possession offenses. The mandate calls for a simple question to be asked and the answer documented in a report: Where did you get the gun?

GunOps Software

GunOps is a software solution, developed by ShieldOps, that works alongside the IBIS system. Using detailed geographic maps, GunOps enables a visual and interactive way to monitor recovered firearm evidence as it is booked into the police department. This allows operators to filter and view firearm related evidence according to geographic areas, which then enables a prioritization of their workload. This is accomplished by connecting many pieces of timely information on firearm crimes, including the results of ballistic examinations that can determine whether the same gun was used in more than one crime incident. The software manages a large volume of information on firearm crimes. For more information go to: www.shieldops.web.officelive.com.

Critical Elements

- Hold regular meetings to share all information developed from inside and outside the gun in taking the presumptive approach with the operational stakeholder partners.

- Leverage output information such as hits, crime gun trace data, fingerprints, DNA, gun crime locations, and types of ammunition used.

- Collaborate routinely with stakeholder partners to improve tactics and strategies and develop new ones to maximize outcome value.

Key Considerations

- Expect the participation of key operational stakeholders at regularly scheduled meetings to ensure that information about relevant tactics and strategies is shared among all appropriate stakeholders.

- Establish the protocol for holding regular meetings with operational stakeholders to share recently developed information and provide updates on follow-ups, making leveraging for more outcome value an agenda item for discussion at the stakeholder meetings.

- Define the types of data (e.g., ballistic hits, crime gun traces, and hot spots) and how it will be managed and integrated into the program.

- Maximize the use of technology for leveragability and sustainability (e.g., electronic mapping and intelligence software).

Summary

The Most Important Thing: Leveraging the various output data (e.g., ballistics hits, crime gun trace data, fingerprints, DNA, exhibit data) so as to improve upon current tactics and strategies, develop new ones, and maximize the crime solving and prevention value for the public.

The Next Step: The next chapter discusses the fundamentals of task number thirteen of *The 13 Critical Tasks*—Improving Programs.

17
Chapter

Task Thirteen:
Improving Programs

Why the Need to Improve?

In the previous chapter, the responsibility for continuous improvement of the day-to-day operations required when taking the presumptive approach fell squarely on the shoulders of the tactically oriented operational stakeholders. This chapter brings that responsibility full circle; back to the strategically oriented policy stakeholders who were implicated in task number one of *The 13 Critical Tasks*—Managing Stakeholders. Both groups must meet at this juncture.

Improvements can best be identified by collecting feedback from each of the stakeholders. Their concerns must be addressed or the program will be inefficient and may even fail.

When any new program is implemented, "bumps in the road" are to be expected. They must be anticipated; they are not excuses to stop, but rather represent opportunities to become better. To reinforce this point, consider the case study below.

A Case Study: Trinidad and Tobago

During the first 26 months of operation of the IBIS system, personnel at Trinidad and Tobago's Forensic Science Centre were disappointed that only 11 ballistic evidence matches had been generated and confirmed. Questions were raised about the value of the government's crime fighting investments. A collaborative effort was launched to improve the ballistics program. Attention centered on the increased workloads caused by rising levels of gun violence, and the mounting ballistic evidence backlog. Staffing levels were a critical issue and it would take many months to recruit and train new people. In the meantime, the backlogs continued to build, causing significant delays that would result in armed criminals remaining free.

Driven by the need for improvement, the Forensic Science Center developed an innovative and two-pronged approach to solving the problem. They began recruitment to increase the number of firearm examiners from three to seven. At the same time, they contracted the services of International Resources Group of Washington, D.C., to provide three qualified firearm examiners for a period of one year. These fully-trained and qualified expert resources were able to immediately begin work on eliminating the ballistic evidence backlog that had grown to over 2,200 cases, ranging from simple firearm possession to murder.

By implementing staffing (people) and process improvements intended to maximize the IBIS technology's potential, the number of confirmed IBIS hits rose dramatically from 11 to almost 300 in just 10 months! One hit gives an investigator leveraging power to develop new leads from no less than two events. Incredibly, the new forensic team observed a hit ratio of about 50 percent on evidence discharged from auto-loading firearms, thus indicating a pattern of repetitive crime gun use. The Trinidad and Tobago case study is an example that program sustainability is dependent upon continuous improvement.

As the case study illustrates, the initial investment of time and attention to developing objective performance measures will provide significant returns in the ability to quickly and accurately focus on real issues, and avoid the time wasting entanglements of misleading perceptions.

While technology applied through good processes can help people make their programs efficient and effective, in the end, only people have the ability to make the decisions and take the actions required to make a program a sustained success.

Recommended Best Practices

New York "COMPSTAT"

As described in earlier chapters, COMPSTAT provides a sustainable method for maximum intelligence sharing based on four tenets: (1) Accurate and Timely Intelligence, (2) Effective Tactics, (3) Rapid Deployment, and (4) Relentless Follow-up and Assessment. It is this fourth tenet that is particularly relevant to this critical task. Follow-up and assessment of results are an essential part of the process. Data is presented on a week-to-date, prior 30 days, and year-to-date basis, with comparisons to previous years' activity. Precinct commanders and members of the agency's top management can easily discern emerging and established crime trends, as well as deviations and anomalies, and can easily make comparisons between commands.

ATF NIBIN Users Congress

ATF established the NIBIN Users Congress that consists of selected representatives from each of the 13 NIBIN regions. The regional representatives gather specific information, such as performance measures and issues of concern, from the NIBIN users within their regions. The information is reported to the NIBIN Users Congress at meetings that are held quarterly or semi-annually. The NIBIN Users Congress has been very effective in improving NIBIN processes and technology.

The graphic below summarizes the continuous improvement cycle:

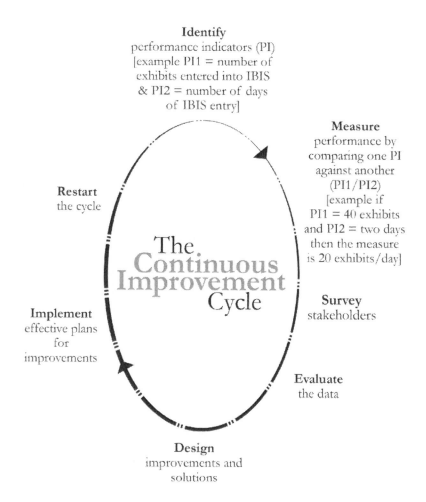

Identify
performance indicators (PI)
[example PI1 = number of
exhibits entered into IBIS
& PI2 = number of days
of IBIS entry]

Measure
performance by
comparing one PI
against another
(PI1/PI2)
[example if
PI1 = 40 exhibits
and PI2 = two days
then the measure
is 20 exhibits/day]

Restart
the cycle

The
Continuous
Improvement
Cycle

Survey
stakeholders

Implement
effective plans
for
improvements

Evaluate
the data

Design
improvements and
solutions

Critical Elements

- Conduct day-to-day, operationally-oriented program improvements through tactical stakeholder collaboration.

- Use performance measures and stakeholder feedback to drive improvements.

- Periodically bring the operationally-oriented stakeholders and the strategically-oriented stakeholders together for program reviews to validate the value of the program outcomes and identify what is working and what is not.

Key Considerations

- Ensure the collection and analysis of continuous stakeholder feedback.

- Ensure the creation of objective performance measures and related reports.

- Institute a regular process for identifying and implementing improvements.

Summary

The Most Important Thing: Conducting regular program improvement reviews to help sustain the program by alerting the stakeholders to problems in a systematic way; some problems and slow success rates in the beginning are to be expected—they are not reasons to stop, but are a challenge to do better.

The Next Step: The next chapter discusses the modus operandi that is vital to the successful execution of *The 13 Critical Tasks*—Regional Crime Gun Protocols.

18
Chapter

Regional Crime Gun Protocols

Why the Need for Protocols?

Many readers may remember a widely publicized murder that occurred 40 years ago in Los Angeles. At the scene of that crime, firearm evidence that was left behind clearly identified the make and model of the murder weapon. For several months, police issued a lookout for the weapon across the North American continent, only to finally learn that the gun had been sitting in the police department's property room all along.

The point of this vignette is not to highlight an oversight of the LAPD—for it is among the most innovative law enforcement agencies in the world today and is one of the most successful at employing the presumptive approach when investigating crimes involving the criminal misuse of firearms. The point is that even today, murder weapons continue to lie undetected in police department property rooms, as was the case 40 years ago when the gun that was used by Charles Manson's cult followers in the Tate-LaBianca murders sat in the LAPD's property room.

Today, the challenge of tracking the gun and its associated evidence in murder and assault cases has become even more difficult. Too often, young criminals rely on guns to settle their disputes and, in the process, frequently travel across police jurisdictions in the course of committing their crimes. In the "thugs-and-guns" world, a vicious cycle exists, as one murder becomes the motivating force for the next. This results in more guns being used in more shootings, thereby generating more evidence and information for the criminal justice system to process. Investigators, forensic laboratories, and criminal justice agencies must keep pace; delays in processing the evidence and in generating the leads that help move investigations forward result in potentially more crimes being committed.

Police must rely upon the actions of police in other jurisdictions to solve cases. A gun seized by police in one city may well be the missing piece of evidence in a murder case being investigated by police in a neighboring

153

city. With gang and gun violence being so regional, the scope of the presumptive approach must be regional as well. Therefore, any sustainable solution must involve the integration of networkable technologies like IBIS and eTrace in order to develop and share crime gun information across multiple jurisdictions within a given region.

A Regional Crime Gun Protocol (RCGP) based upon the presumptive approach can provide an effective and sustainable solution to ensure that valuable information for solving gun related crimes within a particular region makes it back across a city line.

What Is the Protocol?

The RCGP concept was pioneered by ATF, through its Regional Crime Gun Centers in the late 1990s. Officials in Palm Beach County, Florida, worked with local ATF personnel to improve and expand upon the concept by embedding a number of additional protocols within the standard operating procedures of the county's law enforcement agencies.

An RCGP is defined as: A set of predefined and consistent actions taken by police and forensic personnel that are designed to generate maximum actionable intelligence from firearms and ballistic evidence encountered during criminal investigations conducted within those geographical areas in which armed criminals are most likely to be crossing multiple police jurisdictions.

The substance of the presumptive approach is reflected in the two main objectives of the RCGP: The first is to ensure that the valuable information generated from inside and outside a gun is efficiently and effectively extracted from all guns taken into custody as a result of criminal use and possession, and from every piece of ballistic evidence found at a crime scene. This objective will help generate both tactical and strategic intelligence for law enforcement to act upon.

The second objective is to ensure that the intelligence is generated, disseminated, and used by all of the law enforcement agencies within a region that require the information. While a shooting incident may occur in one jurisdiction, the evidence of that incident, such as the murder weapon, may be found in another jurisdiction. It is also common for shooting incidents that happen in one city to spill over into another. Armed criminals routinely cross into neighboring jurisdictions because of habitual travel patterns and other associated criminal activities, such as drug trafficking.

An RCGP is similar to the presumptive approach programs discussed previously and differs only in the respect that it requires the collaboration and agreement of multiple law enforcement agencies within the same "affected crime region"[16] to follow the same crime gun and evidence processing protocols. The regional aspect of an RCGP is designed to avoid situations in which police officers from one police agency continue to search for a murder weapon on the streets of their city while the gun sits unnoticed on the property room shelf of a neighboring police agency. For example, a gun seized from a person in a car stop in the suburbs could be critical to the solution of a case in the neighboring city, and vice versa. This was the situation that Alabama law enforcers faced for six years in the case of Hazel Love previously mentioned in Chapter 2. Here is the story again.

A Case Study: McCalla, Alabama

In March 1996, the Jefferson County Sheriff's Office investigated a home invasion that became a robbery resulting in the murder of Hazel Love, a 68-year-old woman in McCalla, Alabama. Investigators recovered several discharged cartridge cases at the scene and, later, bullets at the autopsy. The evidence was submitted to the Alabama Department of Forensic Sciences lab (ADFS) in Birmingham. IBIS operators at the ADFS lab entered the evidence into the NIBIN database.

In September 2000, police in Adamsville, Alabama, conducted an investigation of a felon who was in unlawful possession of a firearm. At the time, a firearm was retained as evidence and placed on a shelf in the police department's property room.

In December 2002, Birmingham Police investigating a home invasion learned of the firearm stored in Adamsville. Investigators requested a NIBIN check on the firearm. Two weeks later, the ADFS lab surprisingly reported that there was no NIBIN link to the Birmingham home invasion but there was

---

[16] Geographical area in which armed criminals are most likely to be crossing multiple police jurisdictions.

indeed a link between the Adamsville firearm and the 1996 murder of Hazel Love in McCalla. The match was later confirmed by a firearm expert.

In February 2003, the Jefferson County Sheriff's Office arrested two men that were linked to the Adamsville firearm for the murder of Hazel Love as well as for serious crimes across the county. One of the suspects is now serving multiple life sentences without the chance of parole.

This case demonstrates the need for the collection and sharing of ballistic data from crime scenes and firearms seized by police within the affected crime region—until this was done the murder of Hazel Love murder remained unsolved. One department's forgotten evidence is another department's crucial evidence. In this case, neither department knew of the other's evidence.

While the Alabama law enforcers eventually got it right in this case, not all agencies are so fortunate. The presumptive approach is an effective aid in the investigation of gun crime and is optimized when the right people, processes, and technology are in balance and institutionalized within the entire affected crime region. Today, gaps in crime gun tracing and ballistic testing are critical to regionalizing the presumptive approach. For example, many police agencies throughout the United States do not fully utilize NIBIN and eTrace, therefore, they cannot effectively exploit the tactical and strategic value of the information these systems can generate.

As of this writing, police in Alaska, Idaho, Kentucky, Maine, New Hampshire, North Dakota, Utah, Vermont, West Virginia, and Wyoming, do not have IBIS technology within the state. Thus, they may not be making use of, or have ready access to, alternatives, such as public or private NIBIN service providers (e.g., the ATF Lab or IBIS FastTRAX Services).

Some observers may be quick to note that the states mentioned above are not the first to come to mind when one thinks of urban violence. Yet all of them have cities with crime problems involving drugs, gangs, and guns. More importantly, when we consider that a major strength of a ballistic identification network like NIBIN is the fact that it is national, then each state becomes a link in a chain—a chain that is only as strong as its weakest link.

Consider Maine, New Hampshire, and Vermont, which are three of the six New England states. They are linked through interstate highways to major metropolitan areas in Massachusetts and New York, where drug and gang violence is much more prevalent. Just as heat flows from hot to cold, drugs are transported surreptitiously from south to north into the New England region, along the major transportation corridors. Guns and other types of illegal commodities move along these same corridors as well. The gun found during a drug raid in Boston may well represent the "make or break" piece of evidence for police in Providence, Rhode Island, who are investigating a gang-related murder. The reverse is also true. Consider this very plausible scenario: a car bearing New York plates is stopped in Manchester, New Hampshire, for speeding and is then impounded because of an expired registration. It gets towed to the police lot and inventoried. Police find a handgun that has obliterated serial numbers. They charge the driver with the crime and store the gun in the evidence vault. Without a NIBIN check, they have no idea that the gun was used in a murder in New York.

The illustration below testifies to the previous point—it shows a gun recovered in Boston and linked through NIBIN to 14 shooting events with 19 victims. Three of the crimes occurred in other cities within the affected crime region. One of them, involving a victim who had been shot occurred in Rhode Island, and was linked through NIBIN at a time when Rhode Island was still participating in the program.

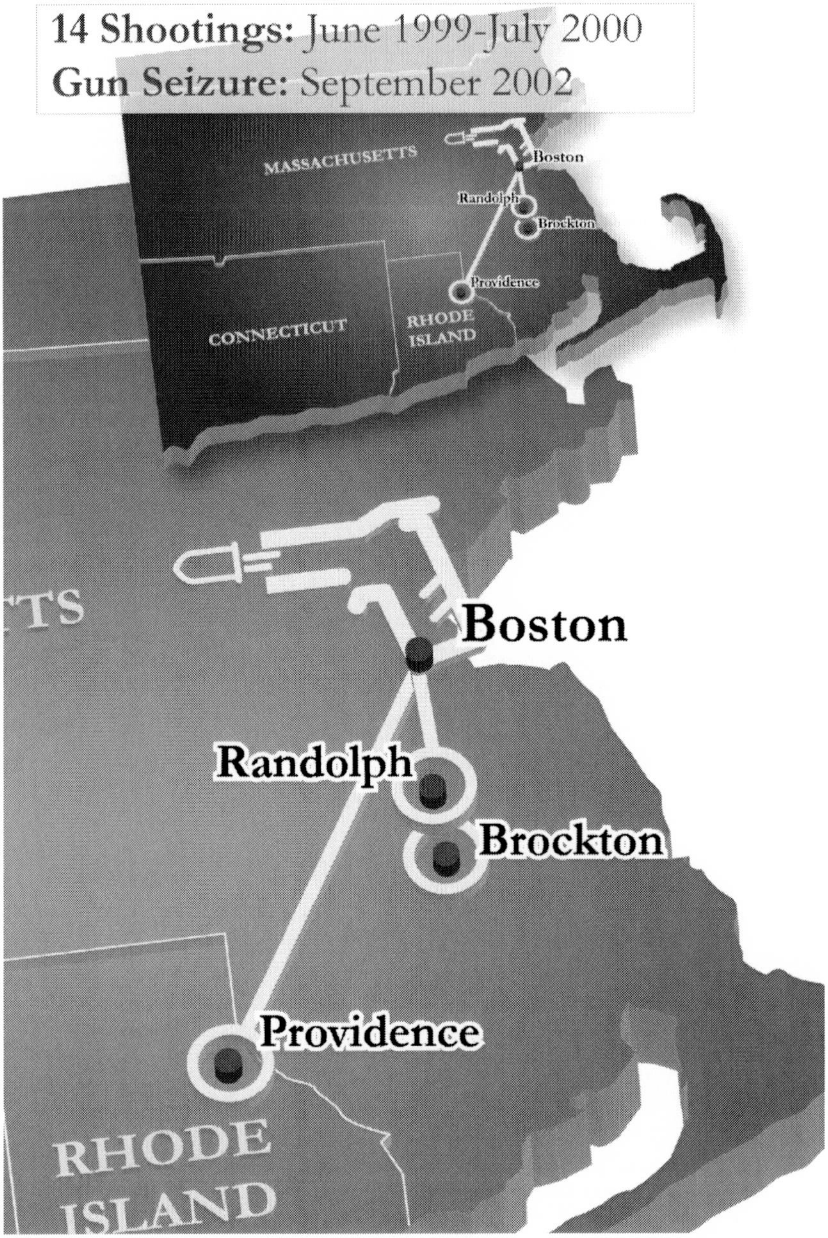

14 Shootings: June 1999-July 2000
Gun Seizure: September 2002
MASSACHUSETTS
Boston
Randolph
Brockton
Providence
CONNECTICUT
RHODE ISLAND
Boston
Randolph
Brockton
Providence
RHODE ISLAND

The illustration makes it clear that NIBIN value is a "two-way street" and that police in both big and small cities can benefit from the information that ballistic networks like NIBIN provides. As in the Hazel Love case, the power of ballistics technology was leveraged across jurisdictions through a network, and this action proved vital in helping police solve her murder.

This is why a small number of police agencies in Kentucky and Maine are doing their best to take the presumptive approach with the help of a few very resourceful and determined champions. They have subscribed to ATF's eTrace and through the use of Project Safe Neighborhoods (PSN) grants, they have outsourced IBIS data input and NIBIN search services through FastTRAX in order to exploit the two most basic types of information generated from inside and outside a gun—ballistic and crime gun trace data.

While gun crime can be generally viewed as a hometown security issue, it can also be seen as a homeland security issue for regions that include certain international borders. A country taking the presumptive approach to collect data on regional cross-border crime will, over time, amass a formidable inventory of data for use in: solving crimes, stopping armed criminals and terrorists, generating intelligence, identifying illegal gun markets, and recognizing crime patterns and trends. This comprehensive data can be used by police and policy makers when designing new strategies and tactics to deal with these cross-border problems.

The timely exploitation of information from crime guns and ballistic evidence that is collected across the various affected police jurisdictions **will lead to more links between guns and crimes and to more shooters identified more quickly.** By identifying shooters more quickly, officers can apprehend them before they have the opportunity to re-offend. Consistently applied protocols serve to institutionalize and embed a sustainable solution within the region served.

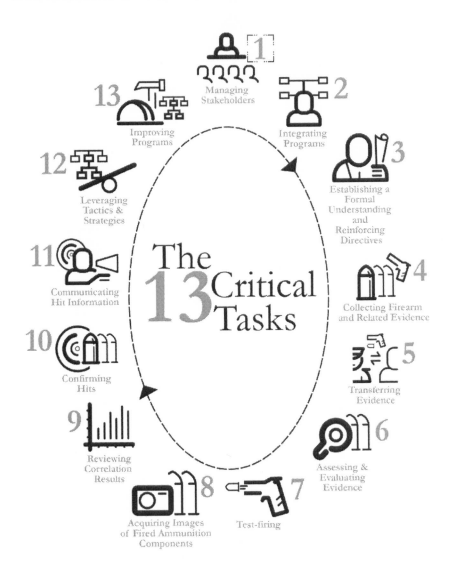

13 — Improving Programs

1 — Managing Stakeholders

2 — Integrating Programs

3 — Establishing a Formal Understanding and Reinforcing Directives

12 — Leveraging Tactics & Strategies

11 — Communicating Hit Information

The 13 Critical Tasks

4 — Collecting Firearm and Related Evidence

10 — Confirming Hits

5 — Transferring Evidence

9 — Reviewing Correlation Results

6 — Assessing & Evaluating Evidence

8 — Acquiring Images of Fired Ammunition Components

7 — Test-firing

Critical Elements

The 13 critical tasks, in balance with people, processes, and technology, can help achieve sustainable firearm crime-solving success across jurisdictions within a given region. The critical elements below will lead to the development of regional crime gun protocols.

- Stakeholder management: Again, as noted in previous chapters, the affected stakeholders must come together as a group.

However, this time, because the area of concern encompasses a region, a diverse mix[17] of representation is needed from across the affected crime region rather than from within a single jurisdiction.

- Gap analysis: An exercise conducted in the latter half of the workshop identifies obstacles and breaks in the current processes, including actions that are not taking place and information that is not being shared. Best practices which have been used successfully by others to manage similar gaps are presented for the group's consideration and adoption as possible solutions.

- Sustainable protocols and substantial benefits: The new crime gun and evidence protocols must be sustainable and have the clear potential to provide substantial benefits. To achieve this, the plan must take the presumptive approach to the investigation of crimes involving the misuse of firearms and must be balanced in terms of people, processes, and technology. One test to help gauge the potential for success and sustainability of the proposed plan of action is to view it in terms of its ability to achieve one or more of the following criteria: (1) provide the stakeholders with new opportunities to solve and prevent crimes committed with firearms, (2) show differentiation from the existing processes—a better way of doing things, (3) change the "rules of game" for all involved.

Key Considerations

- Structured workshop activities: A facilitated workshop would guide the interdependent stakeholders through the thirteen critical tasks in order to stimulate thinking and provide a basis of comparison regarding the ways in which gun crime is currently being approached versus employing the presumptive approach.

---

[17] A mix of participants made up of police, forensics personnel, and prosecuting attorneys from different agencies (including local, state, and federal agencies) within the same affected crime region.

The workshop and supporting materials[18] create a forum for the diverse mix of, on average, about thirty stakeholders to think and act together. To help achieve this, as a public service, Forensic Technology facilitates a series of no-cost *13 Critical Tasks Workshops* for the law enforcement and forensic communities.

- The duration of the workshop: Workshops can be one or two days in length. A one-day workshop can cover most of the issues and deliver an outline of the people, processes, and technology changes that are needed for a new protocol. A two-day workshop would be needed in order to deliver a more-detailed and complete Regional Crime Gun Protocol. The prime concern is the time and availability of the stakeholders. What is often done to maximize their time is that the large group meets for one day and the outline that is produced from that session is turned over to a smaller working group that creates a more detailed and final draft. The coordination of the final draft for comment and acceptance can be handled by mail, courier, email, or fax.

- The identification of the workshop attendees: Attendees should represent line, supervisory, and management personnel that are representative of the affected law enforcement stakeholder groups across the region. The following stakeholder selection guide is provided by Forensic Technology to workshop organizers in order to ensure that the workshop attendees benefit from the perspectives of the stakeholders who possess the diverse skills needed in taking the presumptive approach:

  o Patrol

  o Crime scene processing

  o Investigations (local, state, federal)

  o Special units (Intelligence, Gang, Homicide, Firearm Task Forces, etc.)

---

[18] The *13 Critical Tasks Workshop Workbook*, a self-help guide, is also available free of charge to criminal justice agencies at *www.forensictechnology.com/13*.

- o Prosecutors (state and federal)

- o Property and evidence control

- o Forensics (intake, firearm examiners, fingerprints, DNA)

- o Administrators (senior managers, special program managers, etc.)

- o The identification of the workshop venue: Consider the location and facilities as well as the start and end times. Consider contractual labor issues that may apply.

- o The logistics: There must be a computer projector and a sound system capable of showing Microsoft® PowerPoint® slides and videos with audio tracks on-site. If the venue is large, a public address system may also be necessary. If restaurants or cafeterias are not readily accessible, catering needs should also be considered.

- o The invitation of the participants: Leverage the power of a champion in a position of authority (e.g., Agency head, State's Attorney, U.S. Attorney) and send the invitation under that person's letterhead, with his or her permission.

- o Consider providing participants with Certificates of Achievement if the workshop is considered as part of a recorded in-service training requirement.

Summary

The Most Important Thing: Establishing a sustainable regional crime gun and evidence processing protocol that is in operation across the affected crime region and is agreed to and executed by all law enforcement agencies in the region.

The Next Step: The next chapter describes some techniques for identifying the gaps and balancing the people, processes, and technology needed to create a sustainable crime gun and evidence processing protocol that is capable of delivering substantial benefits to a single locality or region.

19
Chapter

Gap Analysis and Balancing Techniques

Where Are the Gaps?

There are a multitude of activities and interactions which must be properly executed and coordinated across all of the 13 tasks. As with any complex series of activities requiring close coordination, things can sometimes go wrong or "fall through the cracks"—or in other words not get done.

Five years of experience in delivering *The 13 Critical Tasks Workshops* have provided the author with an opportunity to identify recurring patterns which tend to focus attention on certain areas where "gaps" in terms of people, processes, and technology most often occur; gaps where actions can be improperly executed or simply "fall through the cracks" and not be attempted at all.

The areas where the gaps are typically found in terms of people, processes, and technology are as follows.

The "people gaps" can generally be found in four areas:

- Stakeholders

- Communications

- Staffing

- Training

The chart below suggests some key questions to begin the gap analysis.

People Gaps	Key Questions for Gap Analysis
Stakeholders	Who are the champions driving the effort?
	Are all the key agencies represented?
	Are the three key disciplines represented (police, forensics, prosecutors)?
	Is there a mix of line, supervisory, and management personnel involved?
	Is there a continuing forum for stakeholder collaboration?
Communications	Are communications ongoing between the right people?
	Are communications clear and well documented?
	Have the communications been followed-up and are they enforceable?
	Have the problems been identified and discussed?
Staffing	Are there enough qualified people to meet the current workloads?
	Is the lack of staffing delaying processes?
	Will there be enough qualified people to meet future workloads and delivery times?
	Is the staff being used efficiently and effectively?
Training	Does everyone in the program know their role and what is expected of them?
	Can more training improve work quality and expand output?
	Are there opportunities for cross-training and workload redistribution?

The "process gaps" can generally be found in four areas:

- Institutionalization

- Sustainable comprehensive processing

- Actionable intelligence extraction

- Tactical and strategic investigative capital

The chart below suggests some key questions to begin the gap analysis.

Process Gaps	Key Questions for Gap Analysis
Institutionalization	Have the processes been incorporated into the organization's standard operating procedures?
	Are the current processes being enforced and regularly reviewed for follow-up and completeness?
Sustainable Comprehensive Processing	Is the information inside and outside the gun being fully exploited (e.g., ballistics, crime gun tracing, DNA, fingerprints, etc.)?
	Is there, at a minimum, a sustained process currently in place for crime gun tracing and ballistic testing?
	Is the evidence processing being completed in a timely manner to meet the needs of the investigators and prosecutors?
Actionable Intelligence Extraction	Is the output data from inside and outside the gun being analyzed in an efficient and effective manner for maximum actionable intelligence extraction and dissemination to those who need it?
	Is it being done in a timely manner?
Tactical and Strategic Investigative Capital	Is the information from inside and outside the gun being analyzed for its short-term tactical value and long-term strategic value?

The "technology gaps" can generally be found in four areas:

- Ballistics technology

- Other forensic technologies

- Intelligence technologies

- Leveraging data for sustainable crime solving

The chart below suggests some key questions to begin the gap analysis.

Technology Gaps	Key Questions for Gap Analysis
Ballistics Technology	Is there sole or shared access to ballistics technology?
	Is the technology part of a network?
	Is the ballistics technology being fully utilized?
	Are there unbalanced workloads between agencies that use ballistics technology?
	Is the technology keeping pace with modernization advancements?
Other Forensic Technologies	Is there sole or shared access to DNA testing?
	Are there protocols in place to coordinate multiple forensic examinations (ballistics, DNA, fingerprints, and hairs and fibers)?
	Do the current protocols for multiple forensic testing cause processing delays?
	Have these processes ever been mapped?
	What obstacles are faced in accessing these technologies?
Intelligence Technologies	Is the information from inside and outside the gun being mapped along with other demographic crime information for visualization and linkage analysis?
	Are the mapping and data integration processes sustainable?
Leveraging Data for Sustainable Crime Solving	Is forensic output data and crime demographic data being cross-analyzed (e.g., ballistics data and crime gun trace data (the "what" and the "who"))?
	Are cross-data links being leveraged for tactical and strategic use?
	Are relevant regulatory and demographic data systems in place to allow for cross-data links with firearm crime data (e.g., firearm transaction records for crime gun tracing)?

Balancing the Stool

A simple but effective method for helping *The 13 Critical Tasks Workshop* attendees balance the people, processes, and technology involves the use of three flip charts:

Chart One—Processes: On this chart list the proposed new actions or protocols the workshop stakeholders believe need to be carried out under the presumptive approach. For example, the test-firing of all seized crime guns for NIBIN processing.

Chart Two—People: On this chart list the people the workshop stakeholders believe are needed to carry out the listed processes, according to the type of skill required to execute the process. For example, in order to implement the listed process of test-firing all seized crime guns for NIBIN processing, the workshop stakeholders estimate that two additional firearm examiners and three NIBIN lab technicians would be required.

Chart Three—Technology: On this chart list the systems and tools that the stakeholders believe will be required for use by the people who will perform the processes. This chart can also be used to inject technology solutions into the project which have the potential to speed up processes and help make people be more productive. Technology can also help reduce the number of people required to implement a proposed process and help balance the stool.

The three charts provide a flexible and easy-to-work-with visual aid for the stakeholders to use when balancing the people, processes, and technology needed to take a presumptive approach that would work best in their region.

One way to visualize how the charts are used is to consider the actions involved in leveling a camera tripod. Depending on the terrain encountered, you may shorten one leg, extend the second, and leave the third one alone. You continue to adjust, evaluate and readjust the legs of the tripod until you orient the camera in the manner required for the best photo possible under the conditions.

Working the Charts

While facilitating a workshop in 2008, one stakeholder group listed "requirement to test-fire all seized crime guns for NIBIN processing" on the process chart. On the people chart they estimated that the forensics laboratory would need "at least five additional specially-trained personnel to perform the test-firing and data entry".

The stakeholders immediately reached a consensus that the hiring of five additional resources was highly unlikely. On the other hand, the new process to test-fire all seized crime guns for NIBIN processing would be unsustainable without them. As they all stared at the three charts they noticed that the technology chart was blank. That raised the question of whether or not some type of technology could help reduce the requirement for the five additional resources needed to test-fire the seized firearms and process them through NIBIN. The question of technology initiated a discussion among the stakeholders to understand more about the need to hire five additional lab personnel to conduct the process under consideration. They learned that the test-firing process was viewed by some as something that could only be done at the laboratory and therefore the lab would need more people.

Some innovative out-of-the-box thinking on the part of the stakeholders that focused on exploring a technology solution led to the recognition that advances had been made in portable test-firing systems that were safer, smaller, and less costly than a stationary water tank installed in a lab. While working on the technology chart, the group recognized that by acquiring these portable test-firing devices, the test-firing process could be moved outside of the lab and conducted by police officers who worked at the firearm training range and were well-versed in handling firearms. This action would remove the test fire burden from the lab. The lab would then be responsible for only one part of the new process—the entering of the test-fired exhibits into the NIBIN database. Based on this new workload estimate, it was determined that the lab would now only need to hire one new employee to keep up with the data entry rather than five—a number that would prove much more achievable for a sustainable solution. The three charts were used to find a sustainable way to implement the proposed new process by adjusting the balance between people, processes and technology.

Summary

The Most Important Thing: Investing the time and effort required to formulate a regionally focused presumptive approach to the investigation of crimes involving the misuse of firearms by balancing people, processes, and technology for sustained effectiveness.

<u>The Next Step:</u> The West Palm Beach Police (Florida) developed a crime gun processing protocol that follows the presumptive approach to help improve their effectiveness in mounting a response to the rising levels of gun violence in the city. They realized that their sustained success in investigating gun crimes was tied to what surrounding police agencies were doing (or not doing) with their crime gun evidence—the crime patterns in the Palm Beach County area demanded a regional approach. The next chapter provides a case study of the inputs, outputs, and outcomes of the Palm Beach County Regional Crime Gun Protocol Project.

20
Chapter

Palm Beach County Gun Crimes Protocol Policy Recommendations: A Case Study

Overview

This case study provides an excellent practical example of the value of *The 13 Critical Tasks* for use in the development and implementation of a policy like the Palm Beach County Gun Crimes Protocol Policy Recommendations. The Palm Beach protocols strike a balance between the people, processes, and technology required to sustain the presumptive approach to the investigation of crimes involving the misuse of firearms.

How It All Began

Over a five month period between August and December of 2004, a series of shootings took place in West Palm Beach, Florida. The shootings were associated with crimes such as robbery, carjacking, and murder. Four people were murdered within the same week, generating in-depth media coverage. Residents were afraid to venture into the central business district and loudly voiced their public safety concerns to the City Administrators. Police were unable to produce actionable leads through traditional "shoe leather" investigative methods as witnesses were reluctant to come forward. Detectives turned their attention to the use of technology to help them generate actionable information in order to advance the investigation.

Below is a brief synopsis of the events that transpired between August and December of 2004:

- August 29, 2004: Shots were fired during an altercation between young men at a Steak & Shake restaurant. Expended .40 caliber cartridge cases were collected at the scene, entered into IBIS, and searched against NIBIN.

- September 25, 2004: Shots were fired at a local nightclub during an altercation between several young men. Witnesses were uncooperative and would not talk to the police. Fired .40 caliber S&W cartridge cases were collected at the scene, entered into IBIS, and searched against NIBIN. IBIS helped forensic examiners link the evidence to the Steak & Shake shooting the month before.

- November 4, 2004: One vehicle pulled up to another vehicle that was stopped at a traffic light outside an IHOP restaurant. The two men in the first vehicle shot and killed the two in the second. They mistakenly believed that the individuals in the second vehicle were the ones involved in the altercation at the Steak & Shake restaurant. Expended .40 caliber and .380 caliber cartridge cases were collected at the scene, entered into IBIS, and searched against NIBIN. The .40 caliber cartridge cases linked to the August Steak & Shake shooting and the September nightclub shooting.

- November 5, 2004: A gunman shot at a young man standing in front of a Tiger store in Riviera Beach, FL. The shots blew out the store windows but no one was injured. Fired .40 caliber S&W cartridge cases were collected at the scene, entered into IBIS, and searched against NIBIN. The .40 caliber cartridge cases linked to the August Steak & Shake shooting, the September night club shooting, and the double murder which occurred the previous day.

- Later that same day: A robbery was attempted at the Cell Page & Pawn Shop in West Palm Beach, FL. Shots were fired by the perpetrators but no one was injured. Fired .40 caliber S&W cartridge cases were collected at the scene, entered into IBIS, and searched against NIBIN. The .40 caliber cartridge cases linked to the August Steak & Shake shooting, the September nightclub shooting, the double murder, and the shooting at the Tiger store earlier that day.

- November 7, 2004: A drive-by shooting took place on Palm Lakes Boulevard in West Palm Beach. Two men sitting inside their vehicle were murdered in a hail of gunfire. More than forty rounds were fired from an assault rifle and a .40 caliber pistol. Fired .40 and 7.62 x 39mm cartridge cases were collected at the scene, entered into IBIS, and searched against NIBIN. The .40 caliber cartridge cases linked to the August Steak & Shake shooting, the September nightclub shooting, the first double murder, the shooting at the Tiger store, and the attempted robbery at the Cell Page & Pawn Shop.

- November 9, 2004: Riviera Beach police chased a suspect for an incident unrelated to any of the above shootings. The suspect dropped a .380 caliber pistol and eluded police. He was later identified by witnesses. The pistol was test fired and the test fired cartridge cases were entered into IBIS and searched against NIBIN. The .380 caliber cartridge cases linked to the November 4th double murder.

- December 3, 2004: A carjacking occurred at an Arby's restaurant in Palm Beach Gardens, FL. Shots were fired and in the course of the confusion, the suspect dropped a .40 caliber Glock pistol. The pistol was test fired and the test fired cartridge cases were entered into IBIS and searched against NIBIN. The NIBIN check helped forensics experts determine that the Glock pistol was the instrument of the crime in all of the shootings described above.

Knowing that all of the crimes involved the .40 caliber Glock pistol, police were able to leverage the ballistic evidence from each crime with other forensic evidence: fingerprints, DNA, and surveillance video to identify four suspects. Three suspects have pleaded guilty and are currently serving lengthy federal and state prison sentences. The fourth suspect, as of this writing, is awaiting trial.

The Glock pistol used in these crimes had been stolen from the vehicle of a Palm Beach County law enforcement officer in March of 2003. It was traded about a year later to one of the four suspects involved in these shootings in exchange for stolen jewelry.

The People

The arrests in the 2004 spate of shootings helped generate "champions" within the West Palm Beach Police Department who launched a campaign promoting the development of standard protocols for the handling of all firearms and related evidence encountered by the department. The protocols would follow the presumptive approach ensuring that every bit of information held by a firearm or piece of ballistic evidence would be exploited in order to glean its maximum investigative value.

In March of 2005, the Palm Beach County Law Enforcement Planning Council (LEPC), representing all law enforcement agencies operating in the county (city, county, state, and federal) formed a working group to develop enforcement- and prevention-focused solutions to address the rising levels of firearm-related youth violence. Co-chairing the working group were representatives from the police departments serving West Palm Beach, Riviera Beach, and Mangonia Park. The working group received assistance from ATF while developing one of the enforcement solutions which involved the creation of a standard way in which to process evidence and information associated with gun crimes. The gun crimes protocol they developed involved the integration of a variety of tools and investigative aids including: forensics, technology, crime gun tracing, and structured interviews.

To assist the LEPC and its working group with their task, the Palm Beach County Criminal Justice Commission (CJC) hired Florida State University to help collect statistical data on youth violence patterns and trends and to help track the progress and effectiveness of what would be known as the Youth Violence Prevention Project.

Palm Beach County
Criminal Justice Commission

Youth Violence Prevention Project

Courts · Crime Prevention
Corrections · Law Enforcement

OUR MISSION

The Palm Beach County Board of County Commissioners has always been firmly committed to protecting and improving the lives of our young people. A serious threat to their well-being is posed by the proliferation of gang-related crime and youth violence.

When Palm Beach County experienced a significant rise in youth violence in 2004, the County Commission and the Criminal Justice Commission responded by launching the Youth Violence Prevention Project. Commissioners approved $6 million over a three-year period to fund the initiative.

WHY IT'S IMPORTANT

Palm Beach County hired the Florida State University Center for Criminology and Public Policy Research to conduct research regarding youth crime trends. Among other things, the 2005 FSU study found that:

✔ 84 percent of violent offenders have an arrest record before the age of 30

✔ 79 percent of homicide offenders have an arrest record before the age of 30

✔ The largest and fastest growing age group of homicide offenders is 20 to 24 years of age

✔ Five cities were identified as having the highest rates of youth crime: Riviera Beach, West Palm Beach, Lake Worth, Boynton Beach and Belle Glade

Criminal Justice Commission
301 N. Olive Avenue, Suite 1001
West Palm Beach, FL 33401

phone: 561-355-4943
fax: 561-355-4941
www.pbcgov.com/cjc

In November of 2005, the working group drafted the West Palm Beach Gun Crimes Protocol implemented at that time solely within the West Palm Beach Police Department with support from the Palm Beach County Sheriff's Office and ATF.

In June of 2006, a newspaper article in the *Palm Beach Post* set in motion a series of events that would help change the way that firearm crime was dealt with in Palm Beach County.

The article appears in its entirety below.

> ### *Gunned down in Palm Beach County: Many wounded by bullets share two local ZIP codes*
>
> *By Andrew Marra Palm Beach Post Staff Writer*
>
> *Sunday, June 11, 2006*
>
> *A frightening fusillade echoes on the evening news: A golf course manager shot dead in the pro shop. A suburban Lake Worth man gunned down while walking his dog. A teenage cashier shot in the chest by a sub-shop robber.*

Is Palm Beach County really so deadly?

A Palm Beach Post analysis found that while gun violence plummeted across Florida during the past decade, Palm Beach County grew even more deadly. Shooting deaths increased and the cost of caring for the injured ballooned.

Among the findings:

• The county claimed two of Florida's five most violent ZIP codes in 2004, measured by the number of gunshot wounds treated at hospitals.

• The number of people killed by gunfire in Palm Beach County last year remained roughly the same as 10 years before, even as shooting deaths dropped 25 percent across Florida and 48 percent in Miami-Dade County in that time.

• Palm Beach County hospitals billed an average of $55,000 to treat each shooting victim in 2004, up 88 percent from 1994.

• The level of gun violence remained high despite the fact that authorities destroyed more than 7,000 firearms seized by law enforcement officers in Palm Beach County during the past five years.

Palm Beach County's reputation for crime is rising even as many other places are enjoying some of the lowest rates of murder and gun violence in decades.

Last year a national research firm labeled West Palm Beach the 14th-most-dangerous city in the United States — ahead of New York, Los Angeles and Miami, once known as the murder capital of America.

Across Florida, experts attribute a decrease in violent crime partly to state laws that imposed harsher penalties for using firearms during crimes and required violent felons to serve at least 85 percent of their sentences. The decrease came even as the state's population boomed.

Easy availability cited

But parts of Palm Beach County, which have been affected by the same changes, have not experienced the same declines.

"When you factor in the easy availability of handguns to a population that's increasingly violent, it's a major problem," Palm Beach County State Attorney Barry Krischer said. "The challenge for Palm Beach County is reaching out to the at-risk population, getting them to realize that a handgun is not the only solution."

Countywide, deadly gun violence is more widespread than a decade ago. In 2005, at least 173 people were treated for serious gunshot wounds at the county's two trauma centers, at St. Mary's Medical Center in West Palm Beach and Delray Medical Center. That is an increase from the 171 victims treated in 1995.

More people are dying, too. At least 60 were killed by gunfire last year in Palm Beach County, up slightly from the 59 gunned down in 1995, according to the county medical examiner — but far more than the 46 people shot dead last year in Broward County, where the population is 40 percent larger.

The rise in serious gun violence may not seem alarming. But factor in that violent crime dropped dramatically across the rest of the state during the same time period and the contrast is stark.

In Miami-Dade, for instance, the 137 shooting deaths last year were 48 percent fewer than in 1995. Across the state, there were 555 gun-related murders in 2004, 25 percent fewer than in 1994.

West Palm Beach Police Chief Delsa Bush discounted comparisons to other areas and previous years, objecting that killings tend to happen in random clusters.

"There's no rhyme or reason," Bush said. "You can't predict homicides. It goes up and it goes down."

Bush acknowledged, however, that gun violence is entrenched in some of the city's roughest neighborhoods, where the Post analysis shows the number of victims increased from 1994 to 2004.

"The majority of the shooting victims are young black males in a certain age range," Bush said. "They are targeting and fighting each other, and it's a hard thing for us to get a handle on."

Guns are being used in a rising percentage of Palm Beach County homicides. In 1996, firearms were used in 63 percent of the county's killings. By the 2000s, that figure was above 70 percent. What's more, authorities are having a tough time arresting the killers.

West Palm Beach police, for instance, say they have solved just five of the city's 22 homicides last year, although they say they expect to clear others in upcoming months. Officials have attributed their low arrest rate to a reluctance among shooting victims and witnesses to come forward with information.

West Palm Beach Mayor Lois Frankel blamed the shootings that have killed dozens in recent years on the easy availability of guns and an obsession with vigilante justice among young men in the inner city.

Guns, Frankel said, are "too easy to get" in West Palm Beach.

"For every weapon we confiscate, a punk can go get one somewhere else," she said.

Each year, the Palm Beach County Sheriff's Office destroys more than 1,000 guns seized by local law enforcement agencies. Firearms are stolen from cars, businesses, homes.

Many suspects arrested in deadly shootings have felony convictions that bar them from buying a gun legally. Others can't buy a gun because they are younger than 18. But that doesn't mean they can't get one.

"Every young person we've talked to has told us: If they want a gun, they can get one tonight," said Diana Cunningham, executive director of the county's Criminal Justice Commission, which recently published a study on local youth violence.

Shootings are up in the county's most violent areas. So much so that in 2004, two ZIP codes in the West Palm Beach and Riviera Beach areas — 33407 and 33404 — ranked third and fifth in the state for the number of residents treated at Florida hospitals for gun wounds, according to a Post analysis of more than 1,400 gunshot injuries.

Those two ZIP codes occupy Riviera Beach and most of West Palm Beach's north end — neighborhoods long known to be among the most violent in

South Florida. The shootings, drugs and poverty are so pervasive there that residents often seem resigned to their neighborhoods' plight.

"That's how the attitude is now," said Connie Hooks, 27, who is raising three children in her grandparents' small house at 50th Street and Pinewood Avenue in West Palm Beach. "It's sad to feel that way and just shrug your shoulders."

She lives at an intersection where a 16-year-old girl, Angel Brooks, was shot dead in 2004 by two teens with assault rifles after an argument over a scooter. Hooks, who drives a shuttle bus at the Sailfish Marina, hears gunshots some nights. Other nights she hears news of friends or acquaintances getting involved in shootings or brawls.

"I worry about myself being in the wrong place at the wrong time," she said.

The stories of victims caught up in the gunfire abound. A teenage Subway clerk shot during a holdup in West Palm Beach. A 16-year-old girl killed after begging for her life. A man shot in the chest answering his front door. A convenience store clerk murdered during a robbery.

All in the past two months. All in Palm Beach County.

The effects of gun violence can be terrible even when everyone survives.

"Sometimes we are even scared to see a movie," said Gerald Philemond, 30, a computer technician whose two sons were hit by stray bullets as he drove them through Boynton Beach one night in March.

His sons, 11 and 2, survived the shooting. But they bear horrible scars, both physical and emotional.

The 11-year-old, who was struck in the leg, is often too frightened to leave the house. The 2-year-old has a long gash on his neck and a giant bullet scar on his right arm, which is still in a brace and which he may never have full use of.

His sons' medical bills so far have totaled more than $400,000, Philemond said.

Hospital costs surge

The dead and wounded aren't the only ones affected. The cost of caring for shooting victims has skyrocketed.

One example: St. Mary's Medical Center charged an average of $37,500 to treat gunshot victims in 1994, according to the Post analysis. Ten years later, that figure had jumped to $52,800.

All told, Palm Beach County hospitals billed more than $8 million for gunshot victims' medical care in 2004.

The impact doesn't come just in dollars and cents.

At trauma centers, doctors and nurses know all bets are off when a shooting victim arrives. Resources are diverted immediately to prepare the operating room, to ready the victim for emergency surgery.

The emergency room staff can have a patient prepped for surgery in five minutes. But it takes a team of several doctors and nurses, even a respiratory therapist.

"There's a cost to all of this," said Dr. Ivan Puente, director of trauma services at Delray Medical Center. Sometimes the cost is in medical supplies, or blood supplies. Sometimes it hits the other patients square-on.

Often, Puente explained, doctors and nurses must leave less-critical patients when a badly injured shooting victim arrives. For those not on the verge of death, the emergency room becomes a waiting room.

"They will have to wait until we're done with this patient," Puente said.

Palm Beach County taxpayers are shouldering much of the financial cost. The county's health care district, financed by local tax dollars, pays to cover the emergency room bills for uninsured victims of traumatic injuries, including many gunshot victims.

The health care district paid $18.5 million in 1995 to cover costs of treating uninsured county residents in the emergency rooms at St. Mary's and Delray Medical Center. This year, it expects to pay $36.5 million, or roughly $29 for each county resident.

Fears about crime are helping to fuel a dramatic increase in the number of county residents buying licenses to carry guns. Nearly 25,000 county residents owned concealed weapons permits last year, up 72 percent from 10 years ago. During the same period, the county's population grew just 31 percent.

Most firearm owners obtain their guns legally and rarely, if ever, use them outside of a shooting range or hunting trip. But the chasm between law-abiding gun owners and armed criminals is far from seamless.

Firearms disappear from homes, cars and gun stores. They end up at pawn shops, or in the hands of underground dealers — or get passed around until someone tucks one into his pants and robs a bank, carjacks a vehicle or mows down an enemy.

In 2003, a street gang stole a Colt AR-15 assault rifle from the Pahokee police chief's patrol car and used it to rob banks throughout the county. A year later, thieves hit up the Gator Gun and Archery Center west of West Palm Beach, making off with more than 50 firearms. Ten months after that, thieves struck again, taking 68 more guns from the store.

"Every illegal gun was once legal," said Zach Ragbourn, a spokesman for the Brady Campaign To Prevent Gun Violence.

Young black men at center

Politicians, community groups and law enforcement officers have debated for years how to address gun violence, and have created numerous youth intervention programs.

The Criminal Justice Commission says young black men are statistically most likely to be both the perpetrators and the victims of gun violence in Palm Beach County. They are also the fastest-growing demographic in Palm Beach County, according to a commission study.

"That's the age group that ends up being the victims and the perpetrators of these murders," said Cunningham, the commission's executive director.

Criminal justice advocates have recommended that the county and local city governments create youth centers in neighborhoods where some of the most at-risk youths live.

183

*But no one believes gun violence is going away anytime soon in Palm Beach
County. And the costs, in many ways, keep coming.*

Even at the funerals.

*Last year alone, Palm Beach County spent more than $6,900 to bury or
cremate at least six shooting victims — the ones whose families were too poor
to pay themselves.*

After reading this article, Forensic Technology would generate a letter to
the principals identified in the news piece in order to create awareness of
IBIS and NIBIN. In addition, as part of the company's social
responsibility initiative, Forensic Technology would include an offer in
each letter to deliver *The 13 Critical Tasks Workshop* at no cost to the City
and the Police Department. In keeping with this initiative, the following
letter was sent to West Palm Beach Mayor Lois Frankel.

September 7th, 2006

Mayor Lois J. Frankel
200 2nd Street
West Palm Beach, Florida 33401

Dear Ms. Frankel,

I have recently read an article that appeared in the Palm Beach Post entitled "Gunned down in Palm Beach County: Many wounded by bullets share two local ZIP Codes". This article mentions your implication in recent endeavors aimed at halting gun-related violence.

I appreciate the fact that you are adamant about finding innovative ways to address the issue of firearms-related violence, and I applaud your ongoing efforts to quell gun violence in your city. As a result, I feel compelled to write to you today because I have some information to provide you with at the end of this letter that may be of value to you.

I obtained some of this information during my 24 year career with the Bureau of Alcohol, Tobacco, and Firearms which ended upon my retirement as the Special Agent in Charge of the New York Division in 1999. Additionally, some of the information was drawn from my seven years of experience as the Vice President of a company called Forensic Technology Inc.; the makers of IBIS - the Integrated Ballistics Identification System.

*I thought you would be interested to know that there are tools available like the Integrated Ballistics Identification System (**IBIS ®**) to help police solve more gang and shooting crimes but it takes people and efficient processes to make them work. IBIS technology can find the "needle in the haystack", suggesting possible matches between pairs of spent bullets and cartridge cases at speeds well beyond human capacity in order to help forensic experts give detectives more timely information about crimes, guns, and suspects.*

To help extend this capability across police jurisdictions, the Bureau of Alcohol, Tobacco, Firearms and Explosives (ATF) administers the National Integrated Ballistic Information Network (NIBIN) connecting IBIS systems in over 225 labs across the country. <u>NIBIN helps police solve shooting crimes and has proved effective in investigations involving gang related violence.</u>

NIBIN depends on the right mix of people, processes and technology applied together at the state and local level. In turn, the state and local NIBIN partners rely on the federal government for programmatic and technological support.

Therefore, NIBIN needs support from all of its key stakeholders: including investigators and forensic experts, police chiefs and prosecutors, public administrators, law makers and the public as well to be most effective.

Violent crime is on the rise – the FBI reports that murders are up almost 5 percent. Some city leaders and crime experts are blaming increased gang violence and the criminal misuse of firearms.

*Every shooting scene and crime gun has a story to tell. A big part of the story lies in the unique markings imprinted on fired ammunition components found at crime scenes. This data must be fully exploited in order to best link crimes, guns and suspects. **IBIS** technology can certainly be an effective tool but it takes dedicated stakeholders applying their efforts through well integrated processes to make the technology most effective.*

*As the developer of **IBIS**, we at Forensic Technology have compiled a workbook detailing critical tasks and best practices that have been field proven by **IBIS** users in 39 countries around the world. The publication entitled the "13 Critical Tasks: Creating an Efficient and Effective Integrated Ballistics Information Network" is available to Police, Crime Labs, Prosecutors and Public Safety Administrators for the asking. It can be a very useful reference in building any violent crime reduction strategy. A PDF copy can be requested at www.forensictechnology.com/13. You can learn more about Forensic Technology at www.forensictechnology.com.*

Yours truly,

Pete Gagliardi,

VP Corporate and Marketing Communications

Within a week or so, the letter to Mayor Frankel had made its way into the West Palm Beach Police Department, through the Chief's Office, and onto the desk of the Commander of the Criminal Investigations Division, Captain Laurie Van Deusen.

Captain Van Deusen wasted no time in contacting Forensic Technology. Her email is shown below.

Dear Mr. Gagliardi,

I had been forwarded the letter written to Mayor Frankel by you, regarding the benefits of NIBIN and IBIS as we work to reduce violent crime. Reference is made within your letter to Mayor Frankel to an article which was published in our local newspaper, The Palm Beach Post, titled "Gunned down in Palm Beach County: Many wounded by bullets share two local ZIP Codes". We do appreciate your interest in this article and your interest in providing to our City information regarding NIBIN and IBIS. We wholeheartedly agree with everything you have stated as to the benefits of both NIBIN and IBIS in our endeavors to quell violent crime.

The purpose of my response is to let you know that throughout our investigations referenced in the newspaper article, we have in fact, very successfully, utilized NIBIN and IBIS which has enabled our investigators to link a multitude of crimes and offenders. Our agency, taking the lead role in this crime spree, would not be close to linking or solving many of these cases referred to in the article, if it were not for the utilization of NIBIN and IBIS and of course, the cooperation of our local ATF agents and personnel from the Palm Beach County Sheriff's Office Firearms Lab, as well as other local, state and federal law enforcement officers and agents.

My division's investigators have spent an enormous amount of hours on these investigations, with court proceedings coming up in the not too distant future.

Per your offer in the letter, Mr. Gagliardi, I am requesting a copy of the publication entitled the "13 Critical Tasks: Creating an Efficient and Effective Integrated Ballistics Information Network". Certainly continual and advanced training provided to our officers is paramount and we hopefully will glean additional information from this publication which will prove beneficial to all future investigations.

Lastly, I would like to learn more about training opportunities which are available regarding IBIS, as our agency has been applauded and recognized for its initiatives with firearms related practices - to include having one of our sergeant trained in the first phase of IBIS. The training afforded to this sergeant was key to the progress made in these referenced investigations. I'll be able to explain further when I speak with one of you. My contact information is below.

187

Sincerely,

Captain Laurie J. Van Deusen
West Palm Beach Police Department
Commander, Criminal Investigations Division
600 Banyan Blvd.
West Palm Beach, FL 33401

The Workshop

The email from Captain Van Deusen initiated a series of discussions between Van Deusen and Forensic Technology staff which lead to the delivery of *The 13 Critical Tasks Workshop* over a two day period at the start of November 2006.

Thirty people from local, county, and federal law enforcement agencies operating within the county and from the State Attorney's Office attended the workshop. Their varied work responsibilities, such as investigations, crime scene processing, evidence management, forensics, and prosecutors, offered several diverse perspectives on the matters raised in the workshop.

At first, some members of the working group seemed a bit skeptical of discussing "the good, the bad, and the ugly" about their crime fighting efforts openly in a group. As the first day of the workshop progressed, they saw that the best practices which they had proudly put into place very much mirrored many of *The 13 Critical Tasks* that were presented. They began to see value in the fact that they now had independent validation to convince superiors that they were on the right track. You could see and hear the interaction and candid discussions about what was and was not working in Palm Beach County.

By the time the workshop ended, the group was surprised and pleased that they were able to openly get to the heart of the issues that affected them and they were able to identify the people, process, and technology improvements that they believed were needed for an effective county-wide gun crimes protocol. The group did not want their work to go unnoticed. The consensus was that the CJC should hear firsthand about the concerns and recommendations raised in the workshop because the CJC is responsible for developing initiatives and coordinating funding for reducing gun violence in the county.

Forensic Technology presented the workshop findings to the CJC on November 3, 2006. The points outlined below were well received by the council.

Participant's Concerns Generated from the 13 Critical Tasks Workshop to Design a More Efficient and Effective Firearms Crime Solving Network in the County

PEOPLE:

- Additional Firearm Examiner resource(s) are badly needed at the County Lab for confirmation of NIBIN hits & general case work.

- NIBIN Data Input Resource(s) are badly needed to support the County Police Departments and to reduce the data input burden on the County Lab Firearm Examiners and to speed NIBIN evidence and test fire correlations for investigative follow-up.

- Every PD should have a designated person or Property and Evidence Custodian to ensure adherence to a County Crime Gun Processing Protocol.
    - o Consider deputizing in order to share resources

- The Youth Violence Law Enforcement subgroup should be impaneled for the long term.
    - o Act as strategic & tactical steering committee
    - o Hold regular information sharing meetings
    - o Conduct routine reviews of what's working and what is not

PROCESSES:

- Develop a County wide protocol for crime gun processing that mirror's the WPBPD Protocol (including NIBIN & Tracing, DNA, and Fingerprints) and review the MOU that will manage and enforce it.

- o Recommend that the lab be involved to provide some training on technical forensic issues

- o Place high priority on processing recovery on stolen vehicles

- Form a multi-agency working group to review the County Lab intake processes in order to identify any training needed for evidence submission, identify bottlenecks, and provide SOP training to affected users.

  - o Consider people staffing for a Walk in Wednesday type firearms unit approach.

- Consider developing new SOPs for providing roving NIBIN Data Input resource(s) for the entry of test fires into NIBIN.

  - o Provide training for the new data input resources.

- Find new and better ways to eliminate the County Lab backlogs in order to be more proactive in generating ballistics matches and investigative leads and to reduce the reliance on hunches for directing ballistics comparisons.

- Meet the need of the County Lab to provide timely investigative information by keeping current with all correlation reviews and confirmation of NIBIN HITS.

- Recommend the test firing of all police weapons for later NIBIN entry if the weapon is ever stolen.

- Recommend the voluntary documentation of the description of privately owned firearms to be preserved in a safe place by the owner for later reference if the gun is subsequently stolen.

  - o Consider providing an envelope in which the owner could store a fired cartridge case from his or her gun.

TECHNOLOGY:

- Take stock of current technology capabilities.

- Identify technology that is needed to help sustain the new processes to be put in place, and to make the people involved most efficient and effective.

  o Consider acquiring remote NIBIN Data entry systems called BrassTRAX for use by large Police Departments (e.g. WPBPD) and the roving data input resource so that increased NIBIN data input does not interfere with NIBIN Analysis activities at the County Lab

  o Consider a remote data analysis station Match Point Plus for the County lab in order to free up the NIBIN system there for more data input.

  o Consider using Uniform County wide DNA swabbing kits

  o Consider County wide crime gun and ballistics evidence tracking & mapping software

  o Consider test firing stations at County Police Departments - Ballistic Buddies

Conclusion: The goal must be to maintain a proper balance of people, processes, and technology.

Following *The 13 Critical Tasks Workshop* and the presentation of workshop concerns and recommendations to the stakeholders (CJC, LEPC, and the Palm Beach County law enforcement agencies including ATF), began the development of a gun crime protocol which was intended to serve as a recommended policy for the handling of firearms evidence among law enforcement agencies operating within Palm Beach County. It was based on the recognition that criminals are mobile and that property, including found property, held by one police agency may be the key piece of evidence sought by another. The new policy recommendations would build upon what the working group had implemented in West Palm Beach and what had been identified in *The 13 Critical Tasks Workshop*. The CJC, presented with a comprehensive and well integrated crime fighting strategy, supported the expanded undertaking with critical funding in the amount of two million dollars for people, technology and interagency coordination.

The Process

All of this work resulted in the development of the **Palm Beach County Gun Crimes Protocol Policy Recommendations** which cover the collection of ballistic evidence, the DNA swabbing and test-firing of all seized firearms, the interface with NIBIN and the ATF National Crime Gun Tracing Center, and more. On February 11, 2010, the LEPC approved the gun crime protocols shown below as the recommended policy for Palm Beach County law enforcement agencies to follow.

Palm Beach County Gun Crime Protocols Policy Recommendations

(More commonly known as the Palm Beach County "Firearms Protocol")

Purpose:

Firearm related crime often crosses multiple jurisdictional areas and, therefore, the mutual sharing of certain types of firearm crime information is important to achieve a coordinated approach to solving these crimes. A comprehensive approach to combating firearm-related crime involves identifying, investigating and arresting armed violent criminals as well as those persons who illegally supply firearms to the criminal element.

The comprehensive and <u>timely submission</u> of all recovered "known and suspected crime guns," and firearms related evidence to the Palm Beach County Sheriff's Office Crime Laboratory for entry into the NIBIN program (National Integrated Ballistic Identification Network.) through the IBIS computer, or by the entry of a casing, by agencies participating in BrassTRAX, through BrassTRAX, will assist in linking and solving shooting-related crimes and generating additional investigative leads. Nothing will take the place of a thorough and well documented investigation. The more timely entries are made into NIBIN or BrassTRAX, by all participating agencies, increases the likelihood of crime linkage to obtain our ultimate goal to solve crimes.

The complete processing and documentation of all recovered guns, both "known crime guns" and "suspected crime guns" (more commonly referred to as 'found guns'), and all firearm related evidence, in conjunction with thorough documentation of case facts and statements made by possessors, associates of possessors, witnesses, and arrestees, produces stronger cases, <u>often resulting in multi-jurisdictional crime linkage.</u> "Crime plus forensic, equals detection plus conviction." Thorough documentation, processing and forensic analysis is more likely to support a successful prosecution or result in a substantial plea agreement, hence, reducing law enforcement officers' time spent in state or federal court.

As such, the following techniques and procedures are outlined and are intended to be guidelines in the implementation of a multi-jurisdictional and comprehensive approach to combating firearm-related crimes. These guidelines are not intended to replace, supersede or otherwise preclude the application of the Florida Rules of Criminal Procedure and/or Florida Rules of Evidence in any court hearing. They do however supersede previous recommendations and agreements by agencies regarding this policy.

193

Policy Recommendations:

General:

- It is recommended that agencies adopt a policy consistent with these recommendations, and protocols to be utilized when investigating firearm related crimes and incidents.

- It is recommended for all agency issued firearms, issued to personnel, be test fired with two casings maintained by the agency, for NIBIN entry or Firearms Laboratory comparison, if the firearm is stolen from a law enforcement officer, or fired in an officer involved shooting incident.

- A "known crime gun" or "suspected crime gun" is any firearm illegally possessed, used in a crime, or suspected by law enforcement to have been used in a crime. This may include a firearm found abandoned gun, regardless of circumstances, if the recovering law enforcement agency has reason to believe the firearm may have been used in a crime or illegally possessed.

Definitions:

- A "spent casing" is what is ejected from a semi-automatic firearm, or what remains in the cylinder of a revolver after a gun has been fired.

- A "shot shell" is a spent or unspent cartridge fired from a shotgun.

- A "jacket" is the covering of a bullet, which is may or may not be separated from a casing once the gun is fired.

- A "projectile" is the portion of the bullet, covered by the jacket, which may separate from the casing once the gun is fired.

- A "fragment" is a portion of the jacket or projectile which may be recovered when a projectile does not remain intact.

- All known crime guns, suspected crime guns, and other firearms related evidence and items, whenever possible, should be photographed at the crime scene, or location recovered if not a crime scene, prior to being moved, collected, or processed, as photographs may help to develop an investigation, support probable cause, and strengthen the prosecution of those charged with firearms related crimes.

- All recovered "known crime guns" and "suspected crime guns", and all other firearms related evidence should be collected, documented   and considered for forensic examination by the Palm Beach County Crime Laboratory and entry into the National Integrated Ballistic Identification Network (NIBIN), or for BrassTRAX entry by trained and qualified members of the law enforcement agencies who participate in the BrassTRAX Program. The circumstances of each case will determine if the gun and other firearms related evidence or items will initially need to be examined and worked by the Palm Beach County Firearms Laboratory, or if the gun and other ballistics related evidence will remain with the respective law enforcement agency until called for.

- NIBIN entry through the IBIS terminal will be completed by members of the Palm Beach County Firearms Laboratory.

- BrassTRAX entries will be for cases involving the recovery of guns only, or cases in which a single casing was recovered, unless otherwise authorized by the Palm Beach County Sheriff's Office Firearms Laboratory manager or designee. BrassTRAX entries will only be made by trained and qualified members of law enforcement agencies. The Palm Beach County Firearms Laboratory manager, on questionable cases, will have the final authority as to the entry point of a test fired casing or casing(s) recovered at a crime scene or location. When questions exist the Palm Beach County Sheriff's Office Firearms Laboratory Manager should be contacted to discuss circumstances and firearms related evidence and items submitted.

- All guns coming into the possession of any law enforcement agency should be traced through the U.S Department of Justice, Bureau of Alcohol, Tobacco, Firearms and Explosives (ATF) National Tracing Center to assist in Identifying illegal sources of crime guns. This may be accomplished by submitting an ATF Form 3312.1 (National Tracing Center Trace Request Form) via mail or fax to the ATF NTC at the toll free fax number listed at the top of the form, or through the internet based tracing system, eTrace.

- The tracing of all firearms and review of trace results may develop investigative leads, as guns impounded by law enforcement agencies may be unreported stolen guns or guns which are reported stolen to law enforcement but a serial number of the gun was not available by the victim or owner to provide to law enforcement, or the trace results may link individuals with no criminal history who is supplying guns to those with criminal records. Appropriate follow-up investigations of successful traces may too help crime victim in recovering their stolen property and help to solve crimes.

- To perfect a strong prosecutable case and for developing crime gun intelligence, officers at the scene of a crime, or when seizing a firearm for legitimate law enforcement purposes, should ask a series of basic questions of the suspect(s), possessor, or associates of the possessor(s) and/or witnesses to establish gun possession. Obtaining statements from everyone contemporaneous with the incident involving the gun, helps limit or prevent the potential for false alibis at a later time in an investigation, as to ownership, possession, and the source of the firearm.

- Known crime guns and suspected crime guns, when "clear" through NCIC/FCIC should be entered into NCIC/FCIC as "Recovered Guns," as this will prevent another agency throughout the United States from entering this same gun as "Stolen", when an agency already has the gun in their possession. Guns are sometimes recovered during crimes or incidents, prior to a victim or owner realizing a gun has been stolen, or before a serial number is provided to law enforcement for enter stolen into NCIC/FCIC. (See NCIC/FCIC Criteria detailing the specifics of "Recovered Gun" entries.

- Establish processes to ensure all guns entered as stolen, lost or recovered into NCIC/FCIC are accurately entered, which is part of the validation processes mandated through NCIC/FCIC Terminal Agency User Agreements, as inaccurately entered gun information will negate or minimize the opportunity for recovering a stolen or lost gun.

- A copy of teletype entries or clearances for stolen, lost, recovered, or stolen recovered guns, should be included as documents within the original offense, as these serve as excellent references and are important to case investigations.

- Processes should be in place at each agency and within the Palm Beach County to verify the accuracy of gun information entered into NCIC/FCIC. When and if discrepancies are realized, modifications should be made immediately, with copies of the modifications again verified to ensure accurate records. The modified entry, actual teletype copy, should be included in the original report.

Procedures for Processing Known Crime Guns, Suspected Crime Guns, and all other Firearms Related Evidence or Property Evidence:

- Clean latex gloves should be worn when handling any gun or firearm related evidence to prevent cross contamination. Only when exigent circumstances exist should a gun or any firearm related evidence handled without gloves. Exigent circumstances as to why gloves were not worn should be documented in police reports.

- Depending on the case facts and situation, known crime guns, suspected crime guns, and any firearms related evidence or items will be processed for latents and DNA in a manner set forth by the respective law enforcement agencies policies, which are

197

consistent with obtaining the best forensic evidence results. Processing for latents and DNA may be accomplished by agencies Crime Scene personnel, or other properly trained personnel within the agency impounding the gun or other firearms related evidence or items, or by submitting the known or suspected crime gun(s) and other firearms related items or items to the Palm Beach County Firearms Laboratory for processing. Known case facts will determine the need to process or not process for latents or DNA. Exceptions for not processing should be documented in incident reports.

- The recovering department will be responsible for the collection and submission of all DNA suspect/elimination standards to the PBSO Crime Laboratory, when necessary and upon the approval of the Palm Beach County Sheriff's Office DNA Coordinator. All requests for DNA analysis requests must be initiated by telephoning the Palm Beach County Sheriff's Office DNA Evidence Coordinator in advance of any submissions.

- Known crime guns and suspected crime guns should be submitted to the Palm Beach County Sheriff's Office Firearms Laboratory for NIBIN entry, if the agency is not participating in the BrassTRAX Program[19]. Law enforcement officers and agency personnel should not "test fire" any gun in the field, solely for the purpose of determining if the gun is functional; all test firing and function testing will be performed by personnel trained in the handling of firearms, in a controlled setting, such as a firearms range, with all safety practices and protection gear utilized. The "test firing" of all known and suspected crime guns may be performed by any recovering department participating in the BrassTRAX program, where that capability exists, or the firearm may be submitted to the PBSO Crime Laboratory for test-firing

---

[19] BrassTRAX refers to the West Palm Beach Program of remote NIBIN data entry which uses BRASSTRAX-3D technology.

and NIBIN entry when multiple casings exist at a crime scene or location, or when called for by Firearms Laboratory personnel.

- When submitting any gun, "known crime gun" or "suspected crime gun," or firearms related evidence to the Palm Beach County Sheriff's Office Crime Laboratory, the recovering department should complete a Palm Beach County Crime Laboratory Property Receipt for all guns submitted to the Palm Beach County Crime Laboratory. The Palm Beach County Firearms Laboratory Property Receipt should include, when known by the submitting agency, all pertinent descriptive information on each gun submitted; i.e., make/manufacturer, country of origin and importer, model, serial number, caliber, type (pistol, revolver, rifle, shotgun, derringer), finish/color, unique markings or modifications (scope, owner applied numbers), Cyrillic or other unique markings. Information relative to the possessor and associates of possessor (name, alias, DOB, race, sex, identification numbers (driver's license, ID card, etc…), recovery date (crucial), recovery location (be specific), whether the gun is clear NCIC/FCIC or if the gun is a recovered stolen firearm.

- If a gun is known to be a 'recovered stolen firearm,' a copy of the NCIC/FCIC Teletype "HIT "should be attached to the submitting agencies Property Receipt and to the Palm Beach County Firearms Crime Laboratory Property Receipt, or document information as to the entering agency and the entering agencies case number on the Palm Beach County Crime Laboratory Property Receipt, as this information is important for eTrace and further investigation should there be a NIBIN 'HIT."

- If the recovering agency has submitted a trace of the gun to the ATF Tracing Center, the assigned eTrace number or other method used to trace the gun should be documented on the Palm Beach County Crime Laboratory Property Receipt, as this prevents duplication of effort.

- The Palm Beach County Sheriff's Office Crime Laboratory Property Receipt must indicate the type of processing and analysis requested for each gun and other items; i.e., latents, fingerprints, photographing, test firing, and/or just entry into NIBIN. Note if the submitting agency has already processed the gun for latents and swabbed for DNA and NIBIN entry only is required, or other requested Crime Laboratory examination.

- Requests for all firearms related work, to include comparisons related to other cases, should be noted specifically on the Palm Beach County Sheriff's Office, Crime Laboratory Property Receipt, to include the name of agency and the respective agency's case number, along with Crime Laboratory case numbers when known. <u>Requests for firearm related comparison cases will require a call and/or email to the Firearms Laboratory Manager in advance of submissions, to discuss case facts and items impounded which may need to be compared, as it is best for all firearms related evidence to be examined and compared at the same time, rather than separately whenever possible.</u>

- Maintaining control and care over all known crime guns and suspected crime guns, as well as all other firearms related evidence is crucial, as loss of any such items may lead to the suppression of the Firearm Examiners expert testimony which may link the firearm related evidence to the defendant(s) or to other cases dependent upon forensic examinations of firearms or firearms related evidence.

- All guns submitted, regardless of circumstances, should be checked in NCIC/FCIC for information regarding its status as being entered as lost or stolen. The status "Clear NCIC/FCIC" or "HIT", with the entering agencies name and case number noted, should be noted for every gun submitted.

- A copy of the teletype confirmation of an NCIC/FCIC "HIT" record should be included within the original case file, working case file, and a copy attached to the Property Receipt on which the gun is documented upon submission to the respective agencies Property and Evidence Section.

- When a gun is brought to the Palm Beach County Sheriff's Office Crime Laboratory, note on the Palm Beach County Crime Laboratory Property Receipt if the gun is a "stolen recovered gun" or not, the name of the entering agency resulting in the "HIT" and the entering agencies case number. This serves multiple purposes. NOTE: Pertinent information is contained within each entry which may be needed for future reference and may be valuable to an investigation. Once the stolen firearm record is cleared (removed) from NCIC/FCIC, the record will no longer be available, without an arduous off-line search.

Procedures for processing all crime gun related arrests:

- Advise the defendant of his or her Miranda Rights when required.

- The arresting officer should ensure the defendant is fingerprinted if arrested. This will assist in defendant identification at a later date. Whenever possible, if no arrest is made relative to a gun or casing being impounded, a thumb print should be obtained on a notice to appear form, or field interview card/report, if circumstances dictate that a subject will not be transported to a booking facility. Adherence to this process will be of value if a gun is linked to other incidents through NIBIN, latents, or DNA, and when there may be a question as to the true identity of the person encountered and released in the field.

- Request for the defendant to provide a DNA standard. Refusal to cooperate or voluntarily submit a DNA standard should be noted in the report and probable cause affidavit (arrest report.)

- Attempt to obtain a written or taped statement from the defendant, possessor, or associates of possessor, regarding the defendant's or possessor's possession of the firearm; i.e., how the firearm was obtained, when, where and from whom the firearm was obtained. Ask if the defendant or possessor has any prior felony conviction(s). Document all statements by the defendant, whether formal or spontaneous, relating to the firearm and/or criminal record in the police report. Document all refusals by the defendant to provide information relating to the firearm(s). Gun trace results may identify an original retail purchaser. The gun may be an unreported stolen or lost gun or a reported stolen or lost gun when the serial number was not available to the victim/owner to provide to law enforcement when initially reporting.

- Attempt to obtain statements from any witnesses, associates, and accomplices; (i.e., other passengers in a car stop) of the defendant regarding the facts and circumstances of the offense. This assists in establishing the defendant's or possessor's firearm possession, by precluding false alibis by accomplices or associates, claiming ownership of the firearm post arrest.

- Prepare a detailed narrative report as to the circumstances leading to the arrest, or seizing of the firearm, including a complete description of the firearm, make/manufacturer, country of origin, importer, model, serial number, caliber, type of gun, status in NCIC/FCIC (stolen or not. Include complete vehicle information, witness/accomplice information, and a listing all officers present at the arrest. If the arrest began with or involved a 9-1-1 call(s), obtain and preserve a copy of the 9-1-1 call(s) and CAD report(s). If the arrest involved a video-taped traffic stop, obtain and preserve a copy of the recorded encounter. If the arrest involves a foot pursuit, fight or struggle which was audio recorded by the communications center, request and preserve a copy of the tape.

- Obtain a criminal history printout for the defendant and ascertain the number and types of prior felony convictions and ascertain the first date of conviction for a felony. It is important to determine the exact date of the first felony conviction, as this date could be an important factor when charging a Convicted Felon with possession of a firearm, particularly if the defendant's DNA is on a gun, and the gun was reported stolen after the exact date of the first felony conviction. Having this information will help in solidify a prosecution for this charge.

- Use the criminal history information, coupled with the defendant's actions for which you made the arrest, to determine which law violations apply and which venue (Federal or State) provides for the maximum possible sentence.

- Casings entered into NIBIN are automatically correlated to other casings and test fired casings from guns impounded and entered NIBIN, via IBIS or BrassTRAX, throughout our NIBIN Region. If the defendant or possessor is from outside our NIBIN Region, which includes Miami Dade, Broward, Palm Beach and Indian River Counties, all of which have firearms laboratories, request through the Palm Beach County Sheriff's Office Firearms Laboratory Manager, (e-mail, telephone call, or document on Property Receipt), for the test fired casing from a known or suspected crime gun to be "manually correlated" in other NIBIN Regions where the subject may have lived or traveled through, or investigative information suggests the gun was fired during the commission of a crime outside our NIBIN Region. By doing this on a case by case basis, will increase the likelihood of inter-jurisdictional crime linkage. This must be requested; it is not done automatically. The areas or regions of correlation can be expanded at any time after entry into NIBIN, but justification must exist. As an example, if an associate or a possessor, or confidential information says, "possessor shot the gun during the commission of any type of crime in Tucson, Arizona," you may request for the test fired casing to be correlated in those NIBIN Regions between South Florida and Tucson, Arizona (essentially the I-10 east to west corridor.) The Firearms Laboratory Firearm Examiners will handle this aspect.

In order to ensure that law enforcement agencies are aware of the gun crime protocol policy recommendations and that they are understood and followed correctly, a training course was developed by the Palm Beach County Sheriff's Office and ATF which covers several important areas:

- Firearm and ammunition identification, firearm nomenclature, and the ATF eTrace process

- The firearm examination capabilities of the Palm Beach County Sheriff's Crime Lab

- The details of the protocol policy recommendations

- A hands-on practical exercise with various types of firearms

A copy of the training syllabus is shown below.

PALM BEACH COUNTY
SHERIFF'S OFFICE
RIC L. BRADSHAW, SHERIFF

TRAINING DIVISION
****ATTENTION IMPORTANT TRAINING NOTICE****
FIREARMS, AMMUNITION, & PROTOCOL FAMILILIARIZATION COURSE

The PBSO Violent Crimes Division (VCD), in partnership with the Bureau of Alcohol, Tobacco, Firearms and Explosives (ATF), will be hosting a *Firearms, Ammunition and Protocol Familiarization Course* customized for PBSO personnel and other Palm Beach County law enforcement agency representatives. **Representatives from law enforcement agencies from outside Palm Beach County are requested to contact any of the instructors for and invitation or authorization to attend.** This course is essential to improving our endeavors to combat violent crime involving firearms, to increase crime linkage which is likely to increase crime solution. The course has been structured to address the increased volume of firearms being encountered by law enforcement officers in the field, the rise in violent crimes involving firearms, the increase in gang activity, the increase in gun trafficking, tips for increasing recovery of stolen firearms, and the impact firearms related violence has on every law enforcement officer and agency. One of the many intended goals of this course is to improve the documentation of all firearms related identifies, to enhance all processes involving in the seizing and impoundment of firearms to Property and Evidence Sections and the PBSO Firearms Laboratory, leading to the increased investigatory lead when the "Firearm Protocol" is followed. This course is a one day (8 hour) course will be offered at no cost and will be held at PBSO in the 3rd floor CompStat Theater. Course Coordinator: ▨▨▨▨▨▨▨▨▨▨▨▨

Course Dates 2010:
- Thursdays: March 25th, April 22nd, May 20th, June 24th, July 29th, Aug 26th, Sept 23rd, Oct 28th, Nov 18th

Instructors and Topics:
- **ATF / Resident Agent in Charge ▨▨▨▨ (5 hours):** The safe handling and clearing of firearms, proper identification and nomenclature of firearms and ammunition, court room testimony, NIBIN, the ATF Firearms Technology Branch, the ATF National Tracing Center, and other assistance available through local ATF Agents.
- **ATF / Retired Agent ▨▨▨▨ (1 hour):** The ATF internet based tracing system and the benefits to investigations and increased officer safety
- **PBSO Firearms Lab Supervisor / ▨▨▨▨ (1 hour):** NIBIN, BrassTrax, Firearms Laboratory familiarization, submission criteria, and how to make requests for cases to be worked.
- **PBSO Special Projects Coordinator – Firearms / ▨▨▨▨ (1 hour):** The Palm Beach County "Firearms Protocol", Importance of accurate and thorough documentation, Teletype information (stolen, recovered, and recovered stolen guns), Property Receipts and Incident Reports documentation, Success Stories of "Firearms Protocol" processes, Investigative Points of Contact and NIBIN "HITS"

Registration Instructions:
No Cost; No Travel/Training request form is required to enroll. Supervisors or Section Managers and outside agency personnel may contact one of the following Training Unit Clerical Specialists via e-mail to register. Certificates will be issued.

Tools were also developed to allow for better communication of the protocols and the sharing of operational information such as: (A) the

NIBIN hit letter, (B) ATF Publication 3312.12 *ATF POLICE OFFICER'S GUIDE to Recovered Firearms*, (C) Police Notice to Victims of Auto Theft, and (D) ATF Publication 3312.8 *Personal Firearms Record*. Examples of these tools are provided below:

- The NIBIN hit letter: This letter communicates the fact that a NIBIN "hit" has been confirmed to the designated "Agency Investigative Point of Contact" whose job it is to track all NIBIN hits for their respective agencies. It identifies the case information needed to follow-up on the hits. It also denotes responsibilities, requests follow-up and feedback, and provides contact coordinates.

TECHNICAL SERVICES/FIREARMS UNIT
PHONE: (561) 688-4217

2/9/2010

Below is information regarding a Palm Beach County Sheriff's Office Firearms Unit NIBIN "HIT". This report documents NIBIN "HIT(s)" which have been confirmed by the analyst working this particular case(s). The original report documenting and confirming this HIT will be sent to the persons at your respective agencies, as noted on the Palm Beach County Sheriff's Office Property Receipt.

You are being sent this information, as the identified "Agency Investigative Point of Contact", to assist in the furtherance of the investigation into your respective agency case(s). The responsibility is between the recipients of this letter, to review your respective agency case report to determine its classification and status, and further ensure contact is made with the agency or agencies identified in the NIBIN "HIT" report below.

The Palm Beach County Sheriff's Office is requesting that your agencies provides feedback as to the value of these NIBIN "HITS" to the investigations. Please contact Jennifer Stuart, Forensic Scientist Supervisor (688-4217 or stuartj@pbso.org), at an appropriate time, once the investigations are reviewed, evaluated, and either closed or cleared by arrest.

NIBIN "HIT" REPORT

PBSO Case #:   Agency Case #:

Type of Case:

HIT TO:

PBSO Case #:   Agency Case #:

Type of Case:

Forensic Scientist:

Telephone #:   email:

3228 Gun Club Road • West Palm Beach, Florida 33406-3001 • (561) 688-3000 • http://www.pbso.org

---

- ATF Publication 3312.12 ATF POLICE OFFICER'S GUIDE to Recovered Firearms: This publication serves as a ready pocket reference and pictorial on how to identify and describe certain types of firearms for crime gun tracing purposes. It also contains useful firearm related information, such as tips for running database queries on the firearms, the types of people prohibited by law from possessing firearms, and questions to ask persons arrested for firearms possession.

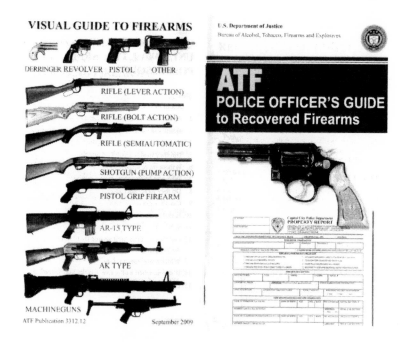

Police Notice to Victims of Auto Theft: This card was developed in response to the common criminal modus operandi (MO) in Palm Beach County which entailed the use of stolen cars as the transportation used in the commission of firearm related crimes and drive-by shootings. The card is left in stolen vehicles that have been recovered and returned to the rightful owners. The card advises the owners on what to do and not do if certain items are missing from or found in the vehicles.

POLICE NOTICE TO VICTIMS OF AUTO THEFT

Recovering Agency Name:_____ Case #_____ Phone:_____

Original Agency Reported to:_____ Case #_____ Phone:_____

→ EXTREMELY IMPORTANT ←

IF YOUR VEHICLE HAS RECENTLY BEEN RECOVERED AFTER A THEFT AND YOU HAVE DISCOVERED EITHER ITEMS MISSING OR ITEMS IN YOUR VEHICLE THAT ARE NOT YOUR PROPERTY, PLEASE TAKE THE ACTION LISTED BELOW. POLICE MAY BE ABLE TO LINK OTHER CRIMES TO YOUR THEFT AND DISCOVER A SUSPECT OR ESTABLISH A CRIME PATTERN.

DO NOT TOUCH ANY WEAPON DISCOVERED, IMMEDIATELY CONTACT AND INFORM THE LOCAL POLICE DEPARTMENT AT ONE OF THE PHONE NUMBERS NOTED ABOVE OR CALL 911

MAKE A NOTE OF ANY PERSONAL ITEMS MISSING FROM YOUR VEHICLE, AS YOUR ITEMS MAY PROVIDE LAW ENFORCEMENT A LINK TO SOLVE OTHER CRIMES.

FURTHER, MAKE NOTE OF ALL ITEMS WHICH DO NOT BELONG TO YOU. TRY TO HANDLE ITEMS AS LITTLE AS POSSIBLE, USING CLEAN GLOVES OR A CLOTH IF NECESSARY.

CONTACT THE LAW ENFORCEMENT AGENCY YOU MADE YOUR ORIGINAL VEHICLE THEFT REPORT TO AND INFORM THEM OF MISSING PROPERTY AND ANY ITEMS YOU HAVE COLLECTED. THEY WILL TELL YOU HOW TO PROCEED. HAVE YOUR CASE NUMBER AVAILABLE.

ATF Publication 3312.8 Personal Firearms Record: This record is provided to firearm owners so that they can record complete and proper descriptions of their firearms. In the event that their firearms are ever stolen, they would have an accurate record to refer to when describing the stolen firearms for police reporting and the issuance of stolen property lookouts.

U.S. Department of Justice
Bureau of Alcohol, Tobacco, Firearms and Explosives
National Tracing Center

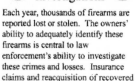 Lost/Stolen Firearms Investigations

Each year, thousands of firearms are reported lost or stolen. The owners' ability to adequately identify these firearms is central to law enforcement's ability to investigate these crimes and losses. Insurance claims and reacquisition of recovered firearms will also hinge on the ability to correctly identify these firearms.

By completing this record and maintaining it in a safe location, separate from your firearms, you will be taking an important first step in the effort to prevent thefts and to keep firearms out of the hands of criminals.

Remember:

"A stolen gun threatens everyone."

Personal Firearms Record

Keep this list separate from your firearms to assist police in the event your firearms are ever lost or stolen.

ATF Publication 3312.8
Revised December 2003

Case Examples

In effect in West Palm Beach and several surrounding towns for over two years now, the gun crimes protocols are delivering multiple benefits for the stakeholders involved. Multiple NIBIN hits have been generated, linking shooting events and firearms to crimes not only crossing multiple police jurisdictions within the county but between counties as well. Here are but a few examples.

Riviera Beach

Police in the city of Riviera Beach responded to a report of a shooting into an occupied vehicle and conducted a crime-scene search. Recovered 9mm cartridge case evidence was submitted to the crime lab and processed through the NIBIN database, as per the protocol. In April 2007, a young man was arrested by the Palm Beach Sheriff's Office (PBSO) for unlawful possession of a Smith & Wesson, 9mm pistol. As per the protocol, the firearm was swabbed for the presence of DNA and submitted to the crime lab for test-firing and entry into the NIBIN database. The PBSO notified Riviera Beach Police that the NIBIN search had linked the 9mm pistol that they had seized to the January shooting of the occupied vehicle. Armed with this information, Riviera Beach Police pursued the investigation of the shooting and learned that DNA recovered from the grip and trigger area of the Smith & Wesson pistol belonged to the young man arrested by the PBSO. Police had enough information to link the suspect found in unlawful possession of the firearm in Palm Beach to the shooting into the occupied vehicle in Riviera Beach. As per the protocol, all of this information was shared among the affected stakeholders who agreed that the suspect, an active shooter, could be removed from the community for a much longer period of time if he were to be prosecuted federally as a career criminal, where he would face enhanced mandatory sentencing—the case was turned over to ATF.

This case serves to support the leveraging value of the regular review of all recent shooting data and the various types of information (e.g., intelligence, forensic, etc.) known about them.

Clubgoers

A victim was murdered in a shooting incident at a local Latin bar in West Palm Beach. Few leads were developed and the case was well on its way to going "cold". One fired cartridge case was recovered, entered into

IBIS, and searched against the NIBIN database. About two months later in Miami, two women walking dogs in different locations were robbed at gun point. A description of the vehicle involved was broadcast to police agencies in the county. Police officers on patrol spotted the suspect vehicle and gave chase. The suspects fired gunshots at the pursuing officers. Police arrested the suspects. The gun was never found but the fired cartridge cases were recovered, entered into IBIS, and searched against the NIBIN database. NIBIN helped forensic experts determine that the gun that was used by the arrested robbery suspects to shoot at police was the same gun that was used in the murder at the Latin bar. This case exemplifies the fact that a collaborative group of stakeholders, executing an institutionalized process leveraged with forensic technology, can be very effective at responding to cross-jurisdictional gun violence.

The Evidence of One

Police in North Palm Beach recovered a gun during a routine arrest. The firearm was test fired and the test fired cartridge cases were entered into IBIS and searched against the NIBIN database. NIBIN helped forensic experts link the firearm to an armed robbery being investigated by the Palm Beach County Sheriff's Office, to a murder in the City of Boynton Beach, and to several shots-fired incidents which had occurred in the cities of Royal Palm Beach and West Palm Beach.

Miami Arrests

The Palm Beach County Sheriff's Office had been investigating a murder with no promising leads. A piece of evidence from that investigation, a fired cartridge case, was entered into IBIS and searched against the NIBIN database. An officer-involved shooting in Miami two months later resulted in two arrests and the seizure of a gun. The gun was test fired and the test fires were entered into IBIS and searched against the NIBIN database. NIBIN helped forensic experts to link the gun to the murder evidence from Palm Beach County giving the Sheriff's Office new and promising leads to follow on the two subjects arrested in Miami.

Crime Spree Over

A stolen gun was recovered by the Palm Beach Sheriff's Office. It was test fired and the test fires were entered into IBIS and searched against the NIBIN database. NIBIN helped forensic experts link the stolen gun to a shooting in the city of Royal Palm Beach in which the victim was paralyzed. A suspect was arrested and the gun and the offender were subsequently linked to a carjacking and four armed robberies in the cities of Boynton Beach, Delray Beach, and Boca Raton, plus multiple shootings in the city of West Palm Beach.

Lake Park

A murder occurred in Lake Park, FL, and cartridge case evidence was entered into IBIS and searched against the NIBIN database. Later, a gun was recovered by police and test fired. The test fires were entered into IBIS and searched against the NIBIN database. NIBIN helped forensic experts link the gun to Lake Park murder. An ATF gun-trace helped police identify the original purchaser of the gun who had reported it stolen. The gun's owner gave the police a list of people who had been at his home around the time the gun was discovered missing. Police were able to place one of the people on the list at the scene of the Lake Park murder. A confession was obtained from that suspect and a second murder investigation was closed in the process.

The preceding success stories validate the fact that armed criminals are mobile and evidence of their gun crimes are often scattered across multiple jurisdictions. An item of property which appears to hold no particular significance to the police agency finding it can be the case-breaker for a neighboring agency. These success stories are credible proof that a sustainable gun crime processing protocol can prevent important evidence from 'falling between the cracks" and stop criminals from going undetected.

Technology

One of the recommendations arising from *The 13 Critical Tasks Workshop* held in West Palm Beach and supported by the Palm Beach County LEPC was the purchase of an additional BRASSTRAX-3D system so that the West Palm Beach Police could enter their cartridge case evidence and test fire exhibits directly into the NIBIN database in a timely and much more efficient manner.

The addition of the BRASSTRAX-3D technology was intended to help sustain the new Palm Beach County Gun Crimes Protocols by providing two key benefits to the entire process:

- The technology would allow the West Palm Beach Police Department to perform their own data entry, thus speeding up the process of contributing evidence and test fires to the lab and resulting in investigative lead-producing hits. Armed criminals could be identified more quickly and denied additional opportunities to do more harm.

- Historically, the West Palm Beach Police Department had submitted large quantities of firearm related evidence to the county lab and was responsible for a significant percentage of the labs' workload. By using their own IBIS system to enter their cartridge case evidence and test fire exhibits directly into NIBIN, the West Palm Beach Police would remove a significant workload from the shoulders of the personnel at the county lab. The lab could then redirect available time to other priorities, such as the performance of NIBIN data entry for the other Palm Beach County Protocol partners who did not have access to IBIS and NIBIN, and focus on the confirmation of prospective hits from data entered into NIBIN by the West Palm Beach Police.

The success of this tactic was quickly acknowledged. **Captain Pat Maney, who at the time of this writing was the Commander of the Criminal Investigations Division—West Palm Beach Police Department, stated that:** *"Prior to the installation of BRASSTRAX at our Department, all shell casing entries had to be made at the local Sheriff's office. This process not only limited our ability to make entries, but created significant lag time between evidence recovery and entry into the NIBIN system. With the installation of BRASSTRAX we now have the ability to enter casings within hours of recovery or immediately after test firing. The end result; we have tripled the number of casing hits resulting in investigative leads over the same time frame in 2007! BRASSTRAX is an integral part of linking violent, firearm-related crime in Palm Beach County."*

In the course of gathering data for this case study, the author of this book spoke at length with senior investigative and forensic personnel about the use of BRASSTRAX-3D by police to send ballistic data to the forensic lab where it would be reviewed in a more timely and efficient manner. The investigative and forensic managers were very clear that this tactic has clearly benefited all of the stakeholders involved and that they had no problems or concerns about the methodologies employed. They all stated that the technology was easy to use and automatically produced images of consistently high quality. Both the investigative and forensic managers felt that they have been given a tool and a process to help accelerate their work and make them more productive and effective at the same time. The mangers said that they can now have critical evidence electronically submitted to the lab and being worked on in a matter of a few in hours, as opposed to the weeks, months, and sometimes years it used to take prior to the new processes that have been made possible through the integration of the new technology. **They stated that if they were to ever lose this capability it would be a step backwards in their crime fighting efforts.**

A news article from the *South Florida Sun-Sentinel* is presented below to address two essential points of this case study: (1) it identifies the reasoning and value proposition behind the West Palm Beach Police Department's decision to acquire a BRASSTRAX-3D system to perform data entry directly into the NIBIN database, and (2) it summarizes the two double homicide investigations introduced earlier in this case study which served as the initial impetus for the creation of the Palm Beach County Gun Crimes Protocol Policy Recommendations.

"BrassTRAX helps police in Palm Beach County match guns to killers"

By Jerome Burdi | South Florida Sun-Sentinel
May 16, 2008

West Palm Beach – The .40-caliber Glock handgun stolen from a sheriff's deputy claimed the lives of four men in three days and left a trail of evidence in its bullet cartridges, discarded at the murder scenes.

It was a bloody November 2004 in the city.

Two double homicides on Palm Beach Lakes Boulevard, labeled revenge killings by police, prompted outcry and community leaders organized rallies. Police told the public the attacks were planned, not random. The only clue detectives had was that the killer used the same gun in the four slayings.

Detectives solved the case by connecting all the bullets using the National Integrated Ballistic Identification Network, or NIBIN. The database analyzed the distinct markings on each of the bullets — linking them to one gun and one killer.

The case was so successful that West Palm Beach police recently bought BrassTRAX, a camera system that allows officers to capture images of those markings.

"The gun has the fingerprint, it has its own unique microscopic detail," said Palm Beach County Sheriff's Office senior forensic scientist Omar Felix. "That fingerprint is impressed into the cartridge case or on the bullet when it's shot out of the barrel."

When police retrieve bullet cartridges from a crime scene, they analyze and enter details of the markings into NIBIN, the national database. The database will repeatedly search to see if that gun has been used in other crimes.

When officers retrieve a gun, they shoot a bullet into a metal tube called a "bullet catcher." The officer then removes the bullet cartridge and records the markings the gun made in BrassTRAX. That image is then input into the national database.

West Palm Beach police started using the BrassTRAX system — paid for with $100,000 from the county's Criminal Justice Commission — in March. The purchase makes West Palm Beach police the second police agency in the county that can enter bullet cartridge images into the national network.

The Sheriff's Office has used the NIBIN network since 2001 and all the police agencies in the county used to take their bullet evidence there. West Palm Beach's newer technology will help reduce the Sheriff's Office workload and cut the sometimes months-long wait to make entries, officials said.

Riviera, Delray and Boynton Beach police departments are also authorized to input their information into the database using the West Palm Beach Police Department's BrassTRAX.

The West Palm Beach Police Department also enters information from officers' guns into the system in case one is stolen and used, like the deputy's gun that was used in the November 2004 double homicides.

Detectives said those cases — where four men were slain in a hail of bullets from the handgun and two other firearms — are a good example of how tracing a gun or bullets can lead investigators to a killer.

"We had no witnesses, we had nothing except expended shell casings and projectiles from the victims," said West Palm Beach police Detective Donald Iman.

Investigators began comparing those bullets and were able to link them to one gun — the Glock. The bullet evidence was the key to linking Derek Dixon to the slayings.

"It's evidence if we can prove that gun was in one person's hands," Iman said.

Police arrested Dixon as a suspect in a carjacking case nearly two months after the killings. He was charged with the murders based on the testimony of a co-defendant and a recorded conversation from the county jail where he admitted to the murders, according to police reports. In March, Dixon, 22, pleaded guilty to the four counts of second degree murder and is now serving 40 years in federal prison for the killings, which will run at the same time as the 40 years he's already serving for carjacking and possession of a firearm by a convicted felon.

Iman documented how the gun evidence and the national network helped map out Dixon's rampage:

To get the sheriff's deputy's gun from the thief who stole it, Dixon traded some stolen jewelry in a street deal in July 2004.

Using the ballistics database to match the bullets fired at each of the scenes, police traced Dixon's attacks between August and December 2004.

He was later identified from surveillance camera images of a Steak 'n Shake restaurant shooting in August. No one was injured but bullet cartridges were left behind.

On Sept. 25, Dixon fired the handgun after a fight at a nightclub on Okeechobee Boulevard but again no one was injured, police said. Victims refused to cooperate but police found more bullet cartridges.

The first double homicide occurred on Nov. 4 when Dixon thought the victims, Reynold Barnes, 23, and Eddie Lee Gibbs, 26, were the people he was firing at in the Steak 'n Shake incident. After leaving an IHop Restaurant, Dixon fired the Glock handgun and another shooter fired a .380 Beretta, police said.

Gibbs and Barnes were hit at least 10 times and died.

Three days later on Nov. 7, Dixon saw Larry Turner, 23, who he thought tried to kill his brother. He followed a car with three people in it and opened fire in a drive-by shooting. Turner was injured but Ali Jean and Turner Norwood, both 22, were killed and bullet cartridges from the handgun were left behind.

At a carjacking Dec. 3 outside an Arby's restaurant in Palm Beach Gardens, shots were fired and a Glock handgun was dropped at the scene.

It was the one police were looking for.

Crosswalk Analysis

The following chart demonstrates the high degree of consistency that exists between the Palm Beach County Gun Crime Protocol Policy Recommendations and *The 13 Critical Tasks*. It serves as a "crosswalk", allowing the reader to shift back and forth between the protocols and the 13 tasks to compare points of similarity.

The 13 Critical Tasks	Palm Beach County Gun Crimes Protocol Policy
#1—Managing Stakeholders	
Develop at least one senior level champion who has the clout required to drive the initiative to bring all the right people into the process.	Several champions developed: The mayor, the West Palm Beach Police Chief, Captains Van Deusen and Maney, the Palm Beach County Sheriff, ATF, the Palm Beach Law Enforcement Planning Council (LEPC), and the County Criminal Justice Commission (CJC).
Identify and assign participants for the strategic (policy) and tactical (operational) stakeholder groups.	The policy maintains ongoing stakeholder groups (policy and operational), uses agency-designated investigative points of contact and the tactical and strategic oversight value of the Special Projects Coordinator—Firearms (assigned to the Violent Crimes Division of the Palm Beach County Sheriff's Office). The Coordinator—Firearms position was specifically created to help the PBC Sheriff's office implement the protocol throughout the county.
Conduct a facilitated presumptive approach awareness session for the strategic stakeholder working group to generate a broader consortium of champions.	Accomplished by the Forensic Technology letter to the mayor and telephone communications with Captain Van Deusen.
Conduct a facilitated presumptive approach protocol development workshop for the tactical stakeholder working group and transmit recommendations to the senior strategic (policy) group.	Conducted *The 13 Critical Task Workshop* held at West Palm Beach, which focused on taking the presumptive approach, and transmitted results to the Palm Beach Law Enforcement Planning Council.

Plan, develop, and implement a sustainable regional program to generate timely crime solving and crime prevention benefits by taking the presumptive approach when investigating crimes involving the misuse of firearms.	The written policy recommendations are being implemented.
Be prepared to reach out and communicate the new program protocols and expectations to all affected stakeholders.	The policy uses a number of communications: Outreach, protocol implementation training, and special tools.
Establish an ongoing process of performance monitoring between the two working groups to ensure that the initiative is well coordinated and is achieving the intended objectives.	The policy reviews and measures performance. The Florida State University Criminology and Policy Research Center also includes the initiative in regular evaluations.

The 13 Critical Tasks	Palm Beach County Gun Crimes Protocol Policy
#2—Integrating Programs	
Integrate information from the relevant crime programs (such as gangs, crime gun tracing, geo-crime mapping, and gunshot acoustics detectors) including forensic data, such as ballistics, DNA, and fingerprints.	The policy integrates with the Youth Violence Prevention Project of the Palm Beach County Criminal Justice Commission integrating innovative solutions relative to the courts, crime prevention, corrections, and law enforcement. In addition, it integrates other solutions, such as ATF eTrace, forensics, such as DNA and fingerprints, and other programs, such as National Crime Information Center (NCIC) and stolen vehicles.
Leverage inputs, outputs, and outcomes of relevant crime programs.	The policy leverages NIBIN and eTrace outputs and other forensic data, such as DNA and fingerprints, with NCIC stolen firearm and vehicle data, police video and audio intelligence, witness accounts, and ATF's Project Lead Gun Trafficking Analysis Program and Armed Career Criminal Program.
Effectively process program output data for both tactical and strategic uses.	The various data outputs are leveraged with other data to improve the case at hand. This is evident in initiatives such as the "ATF armed career criminal enhancement sentencing" for unlawful gun possessors and strategically as well with programs such as ATF Project Lead Gun Trafficking Analysis Program which tracks patterns and trends to identify illegal gun trafficking schemes.
Eliminate silos and stovepipes	The policy recommendations are models of intra- and inter-agency collaboration with information crisscrossing both internal and external lines.

The 13 Critical Tasks	Palm Beach County Gun Crimes Protocol Policy
#3—Establishing a Formal Understanding and Reinforcing Directives	
Thorough documentation of the program and directives—from high level vision and strategy to ground level tactical execution and day-to-day operations.	The written policy recommendations are being implemented.
The issuance of the policy directives from the appropriate level of authority (agency, administrative, legislative).	The West Palm Beach Chief Law Enforcement Officer implemented the initial West Palm Beach Gun Crimes Protocols.
Formal Memorandums of Understanding to allow for participation in joint operations between various independent stakeholder organizations.	Formal Memorandums of Understanding signed by the Chief Law Enforcement Officer implementing the Palm Beach County Gun Crimes Protocol Policy Recommendations.
An internal review mechanism with senior mangers held accountable for their subordinates' adherence to the directives.	An academic criminology and public policy center tracks performance and progress as well as the Law Enforcement Planning Council and the County Criminal Justice Commission.

The 13 Critical Tasks	Palm Beach County Gun Crimes Protocol Policy
#4—Collecting Firearm and Related Evidence	
Collaborate with affected stakeholders to identify a sustainable and timely process for following the presumptive approach in the collection of information from inside and outside a crime gun by balancing people, processes, and technology.	The Law Enforcement Planning Council, the County Criminal Justice Commission and *The 13 Critical Tasks Workshop* held at West Palm Beach generated consensus among the affected stakeholders for the timely processing of gun crimes and evidence including: Crime Gun Tracing, NIBIN test-firing and data entry, DNA, fingerprints, and processing arrests for gun crimes.
At a bare minimum, there should be a protocol to: (1) test fire all guns taken into police custody that are of certain specified types and calibers that data indicates are the most likely to be used in crime, (2) enter all test-fired exhibits and all recovered ballistic evidence of corresponding calibers through an automated ballistics system like IBIS and network like NIBIN, and (3) trace all guns taken into police custody though an electronic information management system like ATF eTrace or IBIS Firecycle.	The policy recommendations far exceed the minimum standards recommended in this book.
The protocol for data collection should be thoroughly documented and integrated into the standard operating procedures within agencies and through a formal MOU across agencies operating within the same affected crime area.	The policy recommendations do this to an outstanding degree of detail and breadth of scope within West Palm Beach PD and across all of the county partner agencies as well.

The 13 Critical Tasks	Palm Beach County Gun Crimes Protocol Policy
#5—Transferring Evidence	
Map the property taken into custody for processing and identify any gaps and time and distance obstacles that impede the timely exploitation of information from crime guns and related evidence while following the presumptive approach.	*The 13 Critical Tasks Workshop* held at West Palm Beach covered this action plus it is an ongoing effort managed by the Special Projects Coordinator— Firearms at the Palm beach County Sheriff's Office.
Balance people, processes, and technology to design a timely, efficient, and sustainable solution for managing the gaps so as to get evidence from the point of custody to the applicable forensic and analysis units.	*The 13 Critical Tasks Workshop* held at West Palm Beach covered this action. The working group developed proposed unique solutions to manage the gaps (refer to *The Participant's Concerns Generated from the Workshop to Design a More Efficient and Effective Firearms Crime Solving Network in the County*).
Document the new process and implement it as standard policy.	The policy recommendations do this within West Palm Beach PD and across the county partner agencies.

The 13 Critical Tasks	Palm Beach County Gun Crimes Protocol Policy
#6—Assessing and Evaluating Evidence	
Create an early opportunity for the forensic specialist and the investigator to collaborate and exchange timely and relevant information in order to fine tune and help optimize the remainder of the processes.	This is handled willingly by the investigators and the firearm examiners.
Establish the required decision matrix against which case-by-case facts and circumstances should be compared to determine the protocols or next steps to be followed (e.g., additional forensic analysis, scope of correlation, selection of test fire ammunition, and crime gun tracing).	The policy recommendations are very specific.

The 13 Critical Tasks	Palm Beach County Gun Crimes Protocol Policy
#7—Test-firing	
Establish firearm safety and anti-contamination protocols for test-firing purposes.	The Palm Beach Test Fire Protocols address safety and cross-contamination.
Establish ammunition selection protocols for test-firing purposes.	The Palm Beach Test Fire Protocols address ammunition selection.
Ensure that a timely and sustainable process is in place for test-firing guns (e.g., for entry into IBIS) that have been seized by police, including those that have no readily apparent connection to a murder or other serious crime.	The Palm Beach County Gun Crimes Protocol Policy Recommendations do this within West Palm Beach PD and across the county partner agencies.

The 13 Critical Tasks	Palm Beach County Gun Crimes Protocol Policy
#8—Acquiring Images of Fired Ammunition Components	
Training: Proper IBIS training and proficiency is a critical component. The worst possible scenario for the user and the technology provider is to not realize success with IBIS because of improper operation.	All IBIS operators in Palm Beach County have attended and followed the required IBIS/NIBIN training.
Quality Assurance: A quality assurance protocol should be implemented for monitoring the input of both image data and case related data as well.	This is done for image quality.
Continued Adherence to Protocols: IBIS protocols taught during IBIS training are designed to maximize the advantages of the system; therefore, they should be followed. For example, the system allows the capturing of three different types of marks from the surface of fired cartridge cases. All three should be captured in order to optimize the correlation process.	Undergoing review.

The 13 Critical Tasks	Palm Beach County Gun Crimes Protocol Policy
#9—Reviewing Correlation Results	
Training: Acquiring the necessary skills to interpret the IBIS correlation scores and utilize the MATCHPOINT+ analysis tools.	All IBIS operators in Palm Beach County have attended and followed the required IBIS/NIBIN training.
The comprehensive evaluation of the all of the output data, such as the correlation scores for breech face impressions, firing pin impressions and ejector marks, and other case data as well.	Currently reviewing the issue of ejector marks.
An enforced protocol to ensure that the correlation result review is conducted for every exhibit reported and is completed in a timely manner which meets the needs of the investigative and prosecutorial stakeholders.	All correlation reviews are kept up-to-date.

The 13 Critical Tasks	Palm Beach County Gun Crimes Protocol Policy
#10—Confirming Hits	
Trained and qualified firearm examiners who can confirm matches and establish hits.	Firearm examiners in Palm Beach County are trained and qualified in their field and as IBIS operators in Palm Beach County they have attended required IBIS/NIBIN training.
Retrieval of the physical evidence from its storage location in a timely manner in accordance with chain of custody protocols and established laboratory intake processes.	The policy covers this issue.
Reporting of the results of examinations.	The timeliness of reporting is something that the Palm Beach County Protocols have addressed with methods like the NIBIN hit letter and coordination by the Special Projects Coordinator—Firearms.

The 13 Critical Tasks	Palm Beach County Gun Crimes Protocol Policy
#11—Communicating Hit Information	
Collaborate with affected stakeholders on the development and implementation of efficient processes to generate information to link crimes, guns, and suspects, and communicate it to investigators in a timely manner.	NIBIN hit letter and Special Projects Coordinator—Firearms
Create awareness of the process, its value, and the expectations of the stakeholders.	Training by the key Law Enforcement Policy Council and coordinated by the Special Projects Coordinator—Firearms and the Firearms Unit Manager at the Palm Beach County Sheriff's Office and ATF.
Require the investigative follow-up of hits.	The NIBIN Hit letter.
Report on investigative action and hit value.	The NIBIN Hit letter.
Track hits and report them to stakeholders.	Training to all stakeholder partners and presentations at the Law Enforcement Planning Council.

The 13 Critical Tasks	Palm Beach County Gun Crimes Protocol Policy
#12—Leveraging Tactics and Strategies	
Hold regular meetings to share all information developed from inside and outside the gun when the presumptive approach is employed by the operational stakeholder partners.	Monthly North and South County Intelligence Meetings and daily oversight by the Special Projects Coordinator—Firearms.
Leverage output information such as hits, crime gun trace data, fingerprints, DNA, gun crime locations, and types of ammunition used.	Being done as part of the policy recommendations.
Collaborate routinely with stakeholder partners to improve tactics and strategies and to develop new ones to maximize outcome value.	The Law Enforcement Planning Council, the County Criminal Justice Commission and the Special Projects Coordinator—Firearms are tasked with this.

The 13 Critical Tasks	Palm Beach County Gun Crimes Protocol Policy
#13—Improving Programs	
Conduct day-to-day operationally-oriented program improvement through tactical stakeholder collaboration.	The Special Projects Coordinator—Firearms is tasked with this.
Use performance measures and stakeholder feedback to drive improvements.	The Florida State University Criminology and Policy Research Center, the Law Enforcement Planning Council and the Special Projects Coordinator-Firearms are all involved in tracking and measuring these metrics.
Periodically bring the operationally oriented stakeholders and the strategically oriented stakeholders together for complete program reviews to validate the value of the program outcomes and identify what is and is not working.	The Special Projects Coordinator—Firearms, the Law Enforcement Policy Council and the County Criminal Justice Commission are tasked with this.

Conclusion

Regional Crime Gun Protocols are set of predefined and consistent actions taken by police and forensic personnel that are designed to generate maximum actionable intelligence from firearms and ballistic evidence encountered during criminal investigations conducted within those geographical areas in which armed criminals are most likely to be crossing multiple police jurisdictions.

The protocols will produce different benefits for each of the various stakeholder groups served.

For example they can:

- Help crime labs increase productivity and effectiveness.

- Help police and prosecutors solve more crimes and remove more, violent criminals from society.

- Help public administrators and policy makers maintain confidence that sustainable solutions are in place to deal with violent crime.

- Help make a region a safer place for the people who live there.

As demonstrated by this case study, Regional Crime Gun Protocols can be sustained and institutionalized so as to generate substantial benefits for all of the stakeholders through the balancing of people, processes, and technology across all of *The 13 Critical Tasks*.

21 Chapter

The Most Important Thing

The twenty preceding chapters of this book have covered many important things. A strategic planning consultant who provided services to ATF once said: "While there are many things that are important and must be done—there is only **one** most important thing".

It is imperative to identify the most important thing and then reconsider the issue in question from that perspective. This technique helps people to focus on the heart or essence of the issue being considered. Once that focus is clear then it can be supported with all of the other important things that must be done.

The list below represents what this author believes is the most important thing in each chapter. It serves as a ready summary of this book.

- The presumptive approach to the investigation of crimes involving firearms presumes that there is an abundance of data inside and outside every crime gun. When fully exploited, this data can be used to generate actionable information of tactical and strategic crime-solving value.

- The adoption of new crime-fighting technologies and the development of processes are required to maximize their benefits (increased speed and productivity) in order to identify armed criminals more quickly before they have an opportunity to shoot and kill again.

- Balancing people, processes, and technology is not only an objective but is a means of overcoming obstacles and bridging gaps to achieve the goal which, in this case, is to provide sustainable and substantial crime solving benefits to the public.

- *The 13 Critical Tasks* developed by law enforcement and forensic practitioners in consultation with renowned academic researchers to integrate and leverage tactics and strategies provide substantial and sustainable firearm crime-solving benefits to the public in an efficient and effective manner.

- A champion or champions having the power to drive change at the required levels must be developed to assemble the various stakeholders needed for taking the presumptive approach as well as provide and advocate resource support for the people, processes, and technology that will be necessary.

- Program integration is a prerequisite for taking the presumptive approach because of: the diverse groups involved, the programs that are already in place, the quantity and nature of the firearm crime-related data to be collected, and the various methods used to process the data.

- The creation of standard operating directives by the senior law enforcement advances the concept of taking the presumptive approach for which the responsible parties are held accountable.

- The comprehensive collection of the many types of data should be part of the presumptive approach that includes ballistic data, crime gun trace data, DNA, fingerprints, and trace evidence.

- The transfer of evidence and property to the lab must be done in such a manner so as to avoid delays, therefore resulting in a sustainable solution for taking the presumptive approach that meets the timeliness requirements of all of the stakeholders, even if it requires changes to organizational behavior and procedures.

- The fostering of collaborative discussions is required early in the laboratory process to enable the forensic specialist to provide the investigator with preliminary information in a timely manner.

- A process must be set up to ensure the safe collection of test fire comparison exhibits and to select ammunition materials which can optimize the automated comparison process.

- Good quality image data collected from fired bullet and cartridge case specimens in both two and three dimensions help guarantee that the best data possible is generated from the automated ballistic imaging process.

- The IBIS correlation result review process is a crucial deliverable in the overall process. Timely and careful attention must be given to this task and its various elements because if a match is missed a second opportunity may not present itself.

- Trained and qualified personnel must be available to confirm prospective matches (hits) and provide detectives with timely investigative leads.

- Protocols must be established to ensure that hit information is communicated to investigators in a timely manner, that the hits are appropriately pursued, and that crime-solving opportunities are not squandered.

- The leveraging of the various output data (e.g., ballistic hits, crime gun trace data, fingerprints, DNA, exhibit data) should be used to improve upon current tactics and strategies, to develop new ones, and to maximize the crime solving and prevention value for the public.

- Regular program improvement reviews help sustain the program by alerting the stakeholders to problems in a systematic way—some problems and low success rates in the beginning are to be expected. They are not reasons to stop, but represent a challenge to do better.

- A sustainable regional crime gun and evidence processing protocol should operate across the affected crime region and should be agreed to and executed by all law enforcement agencies in the region.

- The resolve and effort required to maintain a regionally focused presumptive approach to the investigation of crimes involving the misuse of firearms by balancing people, processes and technology for sustained effectiveness.

So, while every chapter includes a "most important thing", what is the single most important thing in terms of this book?

Is the most important thing people, processes, or technology? Is it *The 13 Critical Tasks* or maybe the Regional Crime Gun Protocols? Is it ballistics, DNA, or fingerprints? Could it be law enforcement or crime prevention? Harsher penalties or social intervention? More guns? Fewer guns?

Just what is the most important thing?

A clue can be found in the prologue at the beginning of this book. In that section, one murder conspirator trying to calm his jittery coconspirator says: **"they got nothin' on us—all they got is some brass on the floor."**

The labeling of "brass on the floor" as "nothing" much to go on, is quite telling. It tends to indicate that 30 years ago criminals didn't have much fear of ballistic evidence, or of any forensic evidence for that matter, except perhaps for fingerprints. At that time, DNA was still in the research lab.

Today, the situation is very different. Advances in science and technology have helped improve the administration of justice by convicting the guilty and freeing the wrongly accused.

Today, the words "forensics" and "crime scene investigation" are common household terms which lead defense attorneys and juries to demand: "where's the forensics?" While these lofty expectations of forensics in every case can frustrate police and prosecutors, they have served to increase awareness and bring out the best in law enforcement.

So then, you might conclude that the most important thing is forensics after all. Wrong. It is not.

This author proposes that the most important thing is **innovation**—the will to advance, improve, change, and modernize.

The young ATF agent introduced in the beginning of this book pursued innovation and learned a lesson—a lesson that would later be the motivator to help create NIBIN, advocate the presumptive approach, and write this book.

Innovation, in every sense of the word, combined with the will to make it happen is for certain **the most important thing**.

Innovation brought to life by entrepreneurs who founded Forensic Technology and introduced the world to IBIS, which is now helping police in over 50 countries solve more gun crimes.

Innovation explored by scientists and forensic experts in the crime labs.

Innovation hammered out and shaped by the men and women in the police departments and prosecutor's offices who dedicate themselves to finding ways to continually outsmart the criminals and to get them off the streets.

Innovation supported by policy makers and legislators who are expected to address serious social problems like crime and violence, and put new solutions in place.

Last and most important, innovation envisioned by all of us, living and working in our communities, concerned about the safety of our families, friends, and neighbors, who see the need for change and do our part to stand up and speak out for liberty and justice for all.

Innovation is the most important thing. Without it, we will not be able to take the presumptive approach to unlocking the story that every crime gun has to tell. Innovation is the key to making the world a safer place in which to live.